"Which recruiters should I be contacting?"

"How do career marketers and career counselors differ?"

"What can I earn in Seattle?"

If you want answers to these and other questions about your Northwest job search, this is the book that will help you.

Based on hundreds of interviews with placement professionals and career counselors, **Executive Search Firms and Employment Agencies in Seattle** explains how executive search firms work, what employment agencies seek, how to apply for contract work, the role played by career marketers and counselors and the other resources available to those in the Puget Sound job market. To help you market yourself in one of the U.S.'s most desirable areas, **Executive Search Firms and Employment Agencies in Seattle** includes:

• contact information, including web site and e-mail addresses;

• descriptions of the credentials required for the job you want; and

• typical compensation.

Executive Search Firms and Employment Agencies in Seattle also describes:

• search firm and employment agency specialties;

• how to make yourself visible to search professionals; and

• the best resume formats.

Most important, **Executive Search Consultants and Employment Agencies in Seattle** tells you how to sell yourself. Hundreds of recruiters and employers have shared their advice on how to best present yourself—and how to avoid the serious mistakes that can sabotage this job search—and possibly your entire career.

Executive Search Firms and Employment Agencies in Seattle

Linda Carlson

Barrett Street Productions
P.O. Box 99642
Seattle WA 98199
(206) 284-8202

Copies of **Executive Search Firms and Employment Agencies in Seattle** and **How To Find A Good Job In Seattle** are available for $24 for each book (includes sales tax where applicable and shipping). Discounts are available on quantity purchases. We accept checks and money orders. Mailing lists for some chapters of this book will be available in spring, 1998. For a price list, send a self-addressed stamped envelope to the address below or check our web site:

Barrett Street Productions
P.O. Box 99642
Seattle WA 98199
(206) 284-8202
http://www.netcom.com/~jimbeaty/jobsearchtips.html

Introduction

Welcome to the Puget Sound job market! Finding a job in the Seattle area can be a challenge. That's where this book can help.

Especially oriented to the executive, manager or professional seeking permanent, interim or contract assignments, **Executive Search Firms and Employment Agencies in Seattle** also provides countless ideas for those seeking administrative, customer service or entry-level jobs. This book is intended to guide you to the many job-search resources in King, Pierce, Thurston, Kitsap and Snohomish counties and help you determine which services are appropriate for your career—and your budget.

When interviewed for this book, placement and career transition professionals were asked:

What they do—whether they counsel or coach, publish job bulletins, maintain online job databases, or "headhunt".

Those who match candidates with jobs were asked how they find candidates, whether the jobs are permanent or temporary, what skills and experience the jobs require and what candidates can expect to earn.

What these services cost and who pays the fees.

Unlike many other career guides, **Executive Search Firms and Employment Agencies in Seattle** is not a compilation of other directories. All of the information in this book is based on telephone interviews concluded in late 1997. (Information is always subject to change, however; prior to submitting resumes, we encourage you to verify the accuracy of names and addresses.)

We look forward to your comments about **Executive Search Firms and Employment Agencies in Seattle**. Please use the form on page 191 to tell us what you found most valuable.

Acknowledgments

This book and Barrett Street Productions' other job-search titles would not be possible without the generous assistance of hundreds of employers, recruiters, career counselors, relocation specialists and other industry professionals. For each of you who have offered advice for job-seekers, my many thanks. And for those job-seekers who since 1990 have shared their frustrations and concerns about the job search, much appreciation.

Special thanks to those who help ensure these books are successful: graphic designer Virginia Hand and western Washington booksellers and librarians, who critique concepts, provide encouragement and then recommend the books to their customers and patrons.

No acknowledgment would be complete without a word of appreciation for my family, which has endured the trials and celebrated the triumphs of independent publishing along with me since the first job-search guide was nothing more than a concept.

Linda Carlson

Contents

1. Selling Yourself to Recruiters and Employers

What does it take to sell yourself in the Pacific Northwest market? How can you make yourself more visible to executive recruiters? How can you guarantee you'll be the first candidate considered when a job in your field opens up?

Whether you're at the networking, resume or interviewing stage, whether you live in the Northwest or want to move here, this chapter offers valuable advice from search consultants and other placement professionals about how to make yourself more marketable in one of this country's most competitive job markets.

Focus. Before you begin a job search, ask yourself questions like these: Where are you going? What skills do you want to use? What are your values? Make sure you know not only what you can do, but what you want to do.

Making yourself visible. You've got colleagues who brag about how often they're called by search consultants...and it's been months since anyone's contacted you. Or you're in your first or second management position and you'd like to ensure you make yourself visible to recruiters, just as part of building a career network. Here's what recruiters recommend: first, attend your industry or function association meetings and network with the others attending. (But don't go overboard; if you attend too many meetings, people might wonder when you work.) Write for professional journals and local business publications. Do pro bono professional work for local nonprofits and make good contacts with your regular volunteer work. If appropriate, participate in Internet online professional forums.

Contacting search firms. If, after reading *How Executive Search Consultants Work*, you believe your experience matches a search firm's focus, it may be appropriate to call or send a note or resume. Before you send information to a firm, however, consider getting references on it. How is this firm regarded in your field or function? Does the firm work on retainer or contingency? Are contingency searches exclusive to this firm? How many searches has a firm done for the client with which you want to work? Will your resume be shown to prospective employers without your permission?

Remember, too, that search consultants are not in the placement business. Finding you a job is not their job. Neither is critiqueing your resume or helping you network. "Don't call to see if we got your resume...and don't expect us to interview you unless your background happens to fit exactly with a search we're doing right now," said recruiter after recruiter.

Oh, and by the way, recruiters also are not in the business of evaluating your experience and telling you how much more you could be making. Don't contact a search firm if you're simply fishing to see how your current income compares with market rates.

Search consultants are hired by client companies to find candidates who have years of excellent experience, usually in a very specialized job just like the one that's open. Which brings us to:

Making a career change. Don't expect us to help you make career changes, warn search consultants. Recruiters are hired to find perfect candidates, not people who **might** work out. As one recruiter noted, employers can find lots of "maybes" themselves; consultants are hired to find the candidates who score 10 on a 10-point scale.

If you are considering a career change, recognize you're tackling a huge challenge. It's hard to change industries after several years. You'll be better prepared for such a challenge if you carefully analyze your transferrable skills and prospect with creativity. A major career shift often requires several steps; you might first move within your function, but to another industry. Later you may have the expertise to move to another function within the new industry. Or you may use the experience you've gained in an avocation to make a functional shift.

Leaving a large company. Suppose you've been with a very large company for a very long time and now you'd like to make a move. Especially if you're thinking about a smaller organization, recruiters will ask questions such as: How flexible are you? How up-to-date and hands-on are your skills? And how willing are you (and your family) to accept a risk?

Preparing a resume and cover letter. Talk to 20 recruiters and almost every one will have the same complaints about resumes: lies and typos. "Tell me what you did, not what you wish you'd done," sighed one search consultant.

And, recruiters all agree, don't lie, especially about degrees or certification. If you've had 15 years of great experience, but you never finished your B.A., be honest up front. Then a recruiter is prepared to discuss the matter with the client company, to determine whether a degree is a must. Remember, search firms verify degrees and professional licensing and certification before they forward a candidate's resume to a client; lies don't go undetected. (Is it necessary to emphasize that lying to a recruiter will probably end the prospect of working with this recruiter now and at any future time in your career?)

References. Executive search firms check references—lots of references. As one consultant explained, "I want to be able to feel I know this candidate when I present him or her to my client." Some firms check 10 references, others 20. Some recruiters want to talk both to people you've worked for and people who've worked for you, possibly on volunteer projects as well as in the workplace.

If you don't have many colleagues to suggest as references, a recruiter may wonder how active you've been in your field. Why *don't* you know anyone? And if you don't have a professional network, who will you consult if you need help with a problem on your new job?

Suppose you're concerned about what a reference might say. Prepare a search consultant for negative feedback (or a refusal to comment). Especially when you believe unflattering comments are unjustified (a case of sour grapes, perhaps), suggest the recruiter contact other colleagues who can explain what's prompting the unfavorable reference. When talking to the search consultant, you should also emphasize what you've accomplished since you worked with this negative individual.

Search consultants who get negative comments often will place followup calls to the references contacted earlier, to doublecheck on a possible issue. As one recruiter noted, search professionals are looking for common threads in the references' comments. One bad reference usually cannot sabotage a candidate with a pattern of otherwise excellent references.

Gaps in employment. Even in a hot job market, employers can be very conservative about candidates with long periods of unemployment. If you've made several changes or you've been out of work, you need to be able to explain this in a professional manner. At the senior level, a period of unemployment—even for as long as a year—may not automatically disqualify you with some search firms. "But convince us your skills are still sharp," recommended one search consultant.

Frequent job changes. Especially for lower level positions, employment counselors prefer a stable work history. For some, that means three to five years with your last employer. Placement professionals want to see commitment to a job; they're concerned about candidates who changed jobs every few months just for salary increases.

Do you just want to "get out"? Some job changes don't work. Often it's because a job-seeker focuses too hard on getting out of a job and spends too little time evaluating the job he or she is moving to.

Why you left your last job. Recruiters and prospective recruiters don't want to hear how much you hate your current job or how badly you were treated by a former employer. Nor are they interested in detailed sagas of unpleasant personal problems (about the divorce or custody battle that prompted you to quit a job or move, for example). Anticipate questions like "Why are you looking?" and "Why were you fired?" and practice brief explanations. There's nothing wrong with admitting there's a misfit with your new boss or that you've outgrown your old job, but be tactful and positive.

Allow time to grieve for your old job. You can't believe the "dream" job didn't work out. Or you're still grieving for the employer who went bankrupt. Or you're bitter about a merger or downsizing or termination. If you're one of the "walking wounded," get some help before you begin your job search. Don't interview until you feel good about yourself or how you left a job.

So you want to relocate here. Research the market carefully and be prepared to tell recruiters and prospective employers why you're job-searching in the Northwest. Recognize that search consultants grow weary of long-distance callers who say nothing more than, "But it's so pretty out there..."

It's particularly exasperating to deal with would-be Northwesterners who have not even researched their own industry to determine if it exists here. Even if the Seattle area does have jobs in your industry or profession, check market supply and demand carefully. As one search professional noted, "Candidates from out of state expect to see the same shortage of candidates and multiple opportunities that exist in the area where they live now." A related problem: because this area attracts and retains so many highly qualified professionals and managers, salaries aren't particularly high.

If you're considering relocation, take a trip out here. Make sure you understand where the population centers are and how long you'll be commuting if you live in Tacoma or North Bend or Mukilteo and work in downtown Seattle. Research the cost of living: walk through a couple of supermarkets, call schools for tuition rates and ask about sales and property taxes. Check the web, call a real estate relocation department or drive around with the real estate ads and see how housing here compares in cost and quality to your current home. If you can't come for a visit right away, use online cost-of-living indices and calculators to research Northwest living costs.

Or you're considering relocating away from here. When you first speak with a recruiter, you must clarify if you're willing to move. Don't say "yes" if there's any chance your spouse might say "no." You think you'll get an offer so good that your spouse can't refuse? Don't count on it, warn search professionals.

Take telephone interviews seriously. If a recruiter reaches you at a time or location that is inconvenient, don't hesitate to courteously ask to postpone the conversation. When you do schedule a telephone interview, ensure you've blocked out enough time, that you're at the given number at the appointed time and that you've arranged to not be interrupted. If you're making the initial contact, be prepared to tell a search consultant what you're seeking. If you must leave a voice message, be specific.

Present yourself well. Like it or not, when you're in the job market, you're a product being scrutinized by prospective buyers. To ensure you present yourself well, think carefully about your appearance. Look the part you want to get, suggests one recruiter.

That means a professional wardrobe, with formal business attire. Even when it's "casual Friday," even when the prospective employer is a software start-up, that means a suit, said recruiter after recruiter. ("Yes," sympathized one search consultant, "you may be interviewing with someone in shorts and bare feet. But *you* can't dress that way.")

Interviews also require careful makeup, an updated (but business-like) hair style and conservative jewelry. Women should avoid unusually long nails and fabrics that are too sheer; men should check on which employers dislike extremely long hair. Both sexes should remember that Crayola-bright hair and body jewelry are unacceptable in many workplaces and that most recruiters dislike cologne and perfume.

Don't overlook the importance of standard English grammar and vocabulary, good table manners and general courtesy. Be punctual and avoid obscenity and racist or sexist comments.

Prepare just as carefully for an interview with an executive search consultant or employment agency as you would for a meeting with a prospective employer. As several recruiters emphasized, "We have to see how you'll look and behave on an interview."

Research the employer. Whether you're interviewing with a recruiter or the actual employer, do some preparation about the position, the function, the organization and the industry. "It's so easy today with the Internet," pointed out one recruiter. Because such research is so much easier than it once was, a candidate who doesn't prepare will look especially lazy.

Interviewing. Be yourself, recruiters caution, not what you think the prospective employer wants. Don't oversell yourself (that means don't inflate your skills), but don't undersell, either. It's your job to show a recruiter or prospective employer what you've done and then emphasize how the skills you've developed relate to what the prospective employer needs done.

Your questions should focus on the job that's open, even if you're thinking ahead to where it might lead you. Especially at the executive level, recruiters and their clients don't want a job to be regarded as a quick stop before you move on to something else. Another critical error: asking for a job you aren't being offered.

Recognize that most hiring managers are not experienced interviewers. Especially if you'll be meeting with a prospective employer, don't approach an interview passively. Be prepared to take the initiative, to tactfully point out why you're an excellent candidate.

Be sure you know how much time is available for the interview. A 20-minute interview, especially if it's with a panel, will require a different presentation than an hour-long meeting with one individual.

Recognize the importance of second and third interviews. This is an opportunity to confirm the favorable impression you made in earlier interviews and move the prospective employer closer to an offer. You'll probably be interviewing with new people, perhaps along with some people you've already met. Remember that information you provided at the earlier interview may not have been passed along. Assume the new people know nothing about you except what your resume shows; answer their questions and show initiative in your comments with the same energy you did (or should have) in preliminary interviews.

Be prepared to continue asking questions. Especially when you're meeting with individuals, you can ask similar questions of each person. Listening to each's response to questions regarding the organization's culture, plans for growth and major challenges will provide valuable information about both the opportunity and your potential future colleagues.

Show enthusiasm for the job. Let the recruiter and the prospective employer know you're excited about the opportunity. Maybe this won't be the right job or the right company or the right time for you to make a change. But if you demonstrate genuine enthusiasm—for the function, for the employer, for the industry—you later may find yourself recommended for other positions, either with this organization or others.

Be professional. Don't regard any conversation with a placement professional or a prospective employer as a casual opportunity to share personal concerns and opinions. "Don't let your hair down," warns one search consultant, who adds that job-seekers should always think before they speak. Nor is a meeting with a recruiter a social occasion; coyness and flirtatiousness are never appropriate.

The greed factor. Yes, it's important to make sure you "qualify your prospects." If you're a manager and you want a management job, you need to know you're not interviewing for a supervisor or coordinator position. But in interviews your first concern should be determining what the prospective employer needs and how you can meet those needs. Once you've done that, then it's time for the questions about compensation. As one recruiter wisely put it, "Don't talk money until you know they love you."

If most of your compensation has always been salary, make sure you understand the potential value of stock options and other incentive compensation. Be sure you're comfortable with the trade-offs that incentive compensation usually requires. For example, start-ups often offer senior executives stock options and bonus plans—but salaries may be lower and there's almost always a significant risk.

Understand and respect the search process. Whether you're a senior executive who's been asked to meet with a search consultant, an experienced manager handed an application form by the personnel receptionist or an administrative assistant being scheduled for a typing test, be courteous about the screening process. If you try to circumvent it, if you insist you can only speak to the hiring manager, you may be regarded as rude, uncooperative and arrogant. This kind of behavior says, "I'm too special for your process," points out one search consultant.

If you are very young... In most cases, recent graduates should find their own jobs. That's one reason college career centers exist. If you didn't get a job through on-campus interviewing and you haven't been looking hard on your own, recruiters will question your initiative. (And remember, few recruiters handle entry-level positions.)

Maintaining your momentum. You've had one great interview and everything looks promising. But don't relax. There's no guarantee you'll get this job; there might be a better candidate or the employer might decide not to fill the position. However committed you are emotionally to this prospect (and however weary you are of the job search), keep researching opportunities.

Stay in touch with the recruiter. Regardless of your level, whether you're working with executive search firms or employment agencies, let your recruiter know how an interview went. Make sure you return the recruiter's calls promptly at every point during the search process.

And after you get the job: Accumulate samples of your work, sales literature about your products or services and clips about projects you've worked on so that you can document your accomplishments when it's time for a performance appraisel—or that next job search.

2. Resumes That Sell You

What's the single greatest mistake most job-seekers make? Resumes, recruiter after recruiter will agree. A good resume is a job-search basic; very often, it's what introduces you and makes an employer decide whether you're worth an interview. If you're networking your way to a new position, a good resume will enhance the professional presentation you've made in person; in contrast, an unattractive, poorly written resume will raise questions about your ability to handle the job.

What does it take to create an excellent resume? Here's some recommendations from executive search consultants, who may see hundreds of resumes each week:

Make your resume visually appealing and easy to read. Make the margins wide, the type large and attractive and the accomplishments easy to spot in the first few seconds. Remember, the volume of resumes received by recruiters and employers means that a resume usually is reviewed in less than a minute. A weary recruiter is likely to give even less time to the resume riddled with spelling errors and printed in very small type with narrow margins on colored paper.

Be honest. "Tell me what you did, not what you wish you'd done," sighed one search consultant. And don't lie, especially about degrees or certification. If you've had 15 years of great experience, but you never finished your B.A., make that clear in your first conversation. Then a recruiter is prepared to discuss the matter with the client company, to determine whether a degree is a must. Remember, search firms verify degrees and professional licensing and certification before they forward a candidate's resume to a client; lies don't go undetected.

Skip the objective. Or if you use one, make it very specific: "Sales management in the high-tech industry," perhaps, or "Senior investor relations position." If you are applying for a specific opening and you expect your resume to be scanned, use the formal job title or number as the objective.

Don't say too little. Describe the companies or divisions where you've worked, the products or services, the markets served and the volume of business. Spell out your accomplishments: "reduced employee turnover 25 per cent in 1997," "designed direct response marketing program that contributed 10 per cent of company's total new sales in 1996," or "increased product's market share by...". Mention who you reported to, who reported to you and any profit and loss responsibility. If you're a technical person, define the environment (e.g., UNIX, IBM, COBOL) in which you worked in each job. Although older job-seekers are often tempted to delete the dates of their degrees, an executive recruiter needs this information to quickly verify graduation.

Spell out your qualifications. Especially if you're making a career change or you're a college graduate applying for an administrative support job, document the skills you have to offer in the position you seek.

Cover letters should sell you, too. A cover letter should supplement, not repeat, the resume information; it should explain why you're writing, what you offer a prospective employer and how you can be reached. But remember that letters and resumes sometimes get separated in the search process; each piece should have the most important information, including how to reach you.

Don't say too much. "Nobody cares what you did 25 years ago," pointed out one recruiter. In most cases, discuss only the past 10 or 15 years. Earlier positions in the same industry or function might be mentioned, but only by title, employer and tenure. (Avoid irrelevant information: the five years you worked as a dental hygienist before going into computer sales doesn't belong on your resume unless you're applying for a sales job in medical products or services.) Don't get wordy or vague; use action verbs, key words and standard industry jargon so that recruiters can quickly see what you've done.

How long a resume? If you have lots of experience, two pages—but no more. "If your resume is longer than that, it tells me you can't be succinct," observed one search consultant. (One rule-of-thumb for a printed resume: a maximum of one page per 10 years of experience...to the maximum of two pages. Some recruiters for technical contract jobs are more forgiving of long resumes because the information is filed via optical scanner and never seen by a human.)

Skip personal information. It doesn't belong on your resume—or in your work samples. And if you're citing your personal web site as an example of your work, make sure it demonstrates your professional skill. Avoid extremely personal information and pictures (pictures of your baby's birth, for example).

Be professional. Don't try to distinguish yourself by trying to be cute: "What will this letter tell you about me? How can it convince you to interview me?" Avoid references to personal problems (a divorce or death, for example) that are prompting a move or job change.

Use a reverse chronological format. That means your most recent job first, following with earlier jobs in reverse order. Most recruiters and employers will not consider functional format resumes that do not include descriptions of your employment history. Said several: "We round file 'em."

Placement professionals look for stability in your work history. If you've had several positions with the same employer or corporate parent, you'll avoid looking like a job-hopper if you list all of the positions under a single heading for that one organization. For example, after "Bigger, Better & Best, Inc., Kirkland WA, 1990-present," describe each of your assignments with appropriate dates: "Senior consultant, 1996-present..." and then below that, "Consultant, 1993-95..." and then, "Marketing assistant, 1990-93..."

Follow instructions. If you're asked to submit samples of your work or list specific kinds of assignments, do so. Avoid excuses such as, "I just moved and can't find anything." Some recruiters will ask for a salary history as part of a resume. (Others specify the opposite.) If you don't feel comfortable supplying this information, discuss your concerns in person or by telephone with the search consultant prior to submitting a resume; don't simply ignore the recruiter's request.

Use the resume format that's preferred by your search firm. Most recruiters using optical scanners want all contact information at the top. Some want you to follow with a mention of your education and then no more than six bulleted points for a summary. But summaries aren't important to everyone—and they can't be highlighted with bullets if the recruiter uses a scanner. Most recruiters do agree that descriptions of each recent job should be written in sentence fragments with consistent syntax and verb tense. Avoid use of personal pronouns.

Scannable resumes. What works? An easy rule, says one scanning expert, is to use no character that doesn't appear on a standard typewriter. This means no rules (lines), no boxes, no graphics (including bullets), no reverse type, no outline type and no underscoring (underlining). Avoid using boldface or italic type in the middle of a paragraph. Stick to a standard business type face (Times Roman, Ariel or Helvetica are often recommended) in 10 point or larger. Avoid adding in extra spaces here and there and do not justify your type. Use opaque white paper and black ink.

The e-mail resume. Recognize that in this high-tech bastion, most recruiters expect you to also have an electronic resume available. A resume prepared in word processing and then sent as an e-mail attachment will present you far more professionally than one composed as an e-mail message. It can also be spell-checked. But some e-mail systems can't send—or receive—attachments. Find out what your recruiter or prospective employer needs and what your e-mail permits. Or create your resume as a text file in word processing and then paste it in the e-mail resume form available on many recruiters' web sites.

Maintain a quality image through the last line. Some job-seekers run out of space and crowd in the last few entries with a smaller type size, with nonstandard abbreviations or even with handwritten notes.

Proofread. Your word processor's spell-checker isn't enough. It won't catch the wrong word, duplicate words and inconsistencies in style, syntax or grammar. It's also unlikely to highlight punctuation or spacing errors.

Write your own resume. People who work in placement complain about "professionally" written resumes. Too often, they say, these resumes look as if the candidate has something to hide. Most resume services follow a standard format, so an operations manager's resume will read much like that of a sales manager's or a human resources director's or a CFO's.

That doesn't mean you shouldn't get advice on your resume. It's not unusual to need help: it may be hard for you to see how to quantify your accomplishments or how to edit descriptions of your jobs. Certainly most of us could use another set of eyes to check grammar, vocabulary, consistency and spelling. So get some help from your college alumni career service, a professional association mentor, a book, workshop or a career counselor. But make sure **you** create the final product.

The right resume format. There's no one right resume style, but starting on page 14, you'll find some examples of resumes that search consultants like. These resumes are based on materials taken from search firms' files. (All names and addresses have, of course, been changed.) Different consultants have different preferences; the resume format suggested by a technical recruiter would probably not be well received by a generalist firm.

However, note how these resumes—regardless of format differences—all meet search consultants' criteria for content. See how employers are described and accomplishments quantified, technical skills are highlighted and recent experience is emphasized.

A final reminder: these resume formats will require minor modification for scanning or electronic transmission.

SUGGESTED HEADINGS FOR YOUR RESUME

Experience

or

Recent Experience

When you're covering only the most recent 10 or 15 years.

or

[Function/industry 1] Experience
[Function/industry 2] Experience

When you wish to highlight your jobs by function or industry; for example, "Marketing Experience" and then "Publishing Experience" or "Financial Services Experience" and then "Hospitality Experience."

or

Professional Experience
Student Employment

For recent graduates who have little professional experience (an internship and a summer job, perhaps), these headings allow prospective employers to see what experience is relevant to the job sought but also let you show that you've had several other years of work experience.

Education

Graduate degree, school/university, city, state, date of degree

Undergraduate degree, school/university, city, state, date of degree

Noncredit certification, college/university, city, state, date of completion

Continuing Education

Where you can cite significant noncredit training relevant to the job you seek. This should be limited to programs that are well-recognized in your function or industry.

Professional Credentials

The place for professional association and other certification, including CPA, CFP and CMA.

Computer Skills

Candidates for technical positions will provide very detailed information under this or a similar heading. Those applying for administrative support and certain professional positions should indicate their proficiency by platform, software type (e.g., word processing or illustration) and specific programs.

Foreign Languages

List only those languages in which you are fluent. Do not make comments such as "semi-fluent." If you speak a foreign language fluently, but do not write it well, note that.

Consulting

Describe projects and clients. If necessary, explain when clients were merged, liquidated or renamed.

Publications

These might be listed in reverse chronological order, in order of importance or by type of publication (books and then periodicals or by trade publications and then consumer magazines). If you have been published many times or if only a few of your publications are relevant to this job search, substitute "Examples of Publications" for the heading. List the title of your writing, the publication's title, the publisher and the publisher's location (for books), the date and possibly a brief description. For example:

"The Publicity and Promotion Handbook: A Complete Guide for Small Business," CBI Publishing, Boston, 1982 (now merged into Van Nostrand Reinhold, New York). How-to advice on advertising and publicity. CBI's best-selling business title in 1982.

Marketing Architectural Services, a case study in "Services Marketing," Prentice-Hall, Englewood Cliffs, 1984. Textbook edited by a Harvard Business School faculty member.

"Career Search," weekly job-search question-and-answer columns for the *Eastside Journal*, Bellevue, and *South County Journal*, Kent, Wash., 1992-present.

Teaching

Indicate institution, location (if not local), dates, title and any important descriptive information. For example:

University of Puget Sound, 1982-84. Adjunct professor, sales management, Seattle MBA program.

Speeches

As with publications, list in reverse chronological order, in order of importance, by topic or by type of audience. Indicate speech title, sponsoring organization, location and date. For example:

"Making Yourself More Competitive in the Job Market," keynote address to the American Women's Society, Pacific Northwest Regional Conference, Kirkland, May, 1997.

Professional and Community Activities

Many recruiters recommend you limit the information in this section to that which is significant in your field (e.g., leadership positions in a professional organization). Think carefully about mentioning participation in political, religious or advocacy groups; it's always possible that this will offend some prospective employers.

LEIGH OLSEN
400 Main St.
Seattle WA 98101
Home: (206) 633-0001
Office: (206) 440-0002

PROFESSIONAL EXPERIENCE

Washington Medical Center, Seattle, vice president, clinical services, 1984-present.

Responsible for management and development of all clinical support and dietary services, organization-wide programs in quality improvement, risk management, JCAHO accreditation and medical staff relations; active in building a continuous quality improvement culture, external collaborative joint ventures and strategic direction for the organization. Accomplishments include:

New Service Development

Orchestrated development of a 20-bed regional rehabilitation service from inception through state approval to start-up. Service now generates $6 million in revenue and represents 20 per cent of total patient days.

Initiated a new peripheral vascular laboratory service which now generates annual revenues of $250,000, far exceeding budget expectations.

Helped negotiate a seven-hospital partnership to provide mobile magnetic resonance imaging service. In five years, despite competitive environment, venture has expanded to include 10 hospitals and now provides the lowest cost service in this region.

Directed start-up of an industrial mammography screening program, coordinating participation of a large physician practice group, a radiology group, a medical center and a major local firm.

Launched sports medicine rehabilitation center as a joint venture with a physician group, negotiating a lease for $1 per year in a for-profit fitness center.

Problem Solving

Organized a hospital-wide equipment repair insurance program with outside vendor yielding cost savings of $160,000 in one year.

Negotiated agreement with Hospital Auxiliary to transfer management of coffee and gift shops to hospital's food services department, expanding hours of service and achieving cost savings (turned around $25,000 annual loss to $15,000 profit).

Designed food service management competitive bid process which resulted in $50,000 operational savings, improved employee morale and added capital improvements of $25,000.

Valley Hospital, Lincoln MA, chief executive officer, 1976-84; vice president, 1973-76.

Responsible for hospital direction and operations. Accomplishments:

Initiated and completed construction of $9 million hospital facility.

Negotiated sale of former hospital facility for Section 8 housing for the elderly.

Conducted community relations program which received national recognition in "Hospital Administration" magazine.

EDUCATION

The George Washington University, Washington, D.C., Master of Arts in Health Care Administration, 1973

Washington State University, Pullman, Bachelor of Science, 1965

PUBLICATIONS

"Using Community Surveys to Set Hospital Goals," *Hospital Administration*, Jan. 1, 1982

AWARDS

Public Relations Citation, 1981, The Academy of Hospital Public Relations

ROBIN ROSENTHAL
111 Ballard Ave. N.W.
Seattle WA 98107
(206) 789-0000
robinr@provider.com

Experience

Vice President, Operations, Call-Out Inc., Kirkland, 1994-present.
Responsible for manufacturing, software configuration, installation, documentation, training and customer support departments of high-tech start-up making computerized outbound telephone dialing equipment. Instrumental in helping grow the company from less than $1 million in annual sales to $40 million with 20 per cent after-tax profit. Managed the development of systems, procedures and organization necessary to accomplish this growth and complete an initial public offering.

Medi-Search Corp., Tacoma, 1985-93.

Vice President, Operations, 1987-93.
Responsible for all aspects of manufacturing, quality assurance, account ing and administration for this start-up developing a cardiac output monitor...[Edited due to space limitations.]

Director of Finance, 1985-86.
Directed all aspects of finance and administration for rapid growth start-up company, including...[Edited due to space limitations.]

AERO-Control, Renton, 1980-85.

Director of Manufacturing, 1982-85.
Managed 150-person manufacturing operation for $20 million aerospace subcontractor. Responsibilities included... [Edited due to space limitations.]Major accomplishments: reduced production cost of sales by...[Edited due to space limitations.]

Controller, 1980-82.
Responsible for...[Edited due to space limitations.]

Manager, Corporate Profitability Analysis, American Bank, Seattle, 1975-80.

Education

Master of Business Administration, Harvard Business School, Boston, Massachusetts, 1975.

Bachelor of Science, Electrical Engineering, University of Arizona, Tucson, Arizona, 1970.

Military Service

Lieutenant j.g., U.S. Public Health Service, 1970-73.

MCKENNA PHILLIPS
P.O. Box 99000
Seattle WA 98199
Phone: (206) 284-0000/Fax: (206) 285-0000
phillips@nwproman.com

EXPERIENCE SUMMARY

Consulted on and managed the development of a mortgage loan documentation processing system.

Identified and developed technology solution markets for a major CASE tool vendor providing technical support for clients engaged in migration of mainframe legacy systems to client server technology.

Managed a project team for a major telecommunications corporation assigned to define personnel and technical resources required to build a custom system development methodology around information engineering methods and techniques.

METHODOLOGY/CASE TOOL SUMMARY

James Martin's IE-Expert Information Engineering Methodology; Ernst & Young's Navigator Information Engineering Methodology; Arthur Andersen's Method 1

TECHNOLOGY SUMMARY

486 PCs; MS-DOS; MS Windows; MS Office; IBM 3090-308Xs; COM-PLETE; MVS/SP; COBOL; Datamanager; Adabas.

EDUCATION AND TECHNICAL TRAINING

Central Washington University, Ellensburg, B.A. Business Administration (Accounting), with honors, 1976.

KnowledgeWare's CASE Tool Workstations (IEW/ADW) and Texas Instruments' Information Engineering Facility (IEF).

WORK HISTORY

1992-present, Bigger & Best Mortgage Co., Lynnwood WA, project manager/ consultant

Responsibilities include management of loan processing operations to support development of user requirements for a new mortgage loan documentation processing system. Used James Martin's Information Engineering Technology following Ernst & Young's Navigator Information Engineering Methodology to develop a business area analysis with a high-level enterprise data model and detailed function/process models. New processing system based on these models significantly improved quality of the loan processing function and, for the first time, provided timely loan status information to the processing staff, loan officers, executive management and real estate agent customer base...[Edited due to space limitations.]

3. How Executive Search Consultants Work

Executive search firms serve as consultants, usually to larger employers which are creating new executive-level positions, replacing an executive or making a significant change (perhaps due to merger or downsizing) in the organization's senior management. Search firms work for the client companies, usually on a retainer or contingency basis.

The largest and best-known search firms work only on a retained basis, meaning they are paid for their work whether or not a position is filled. In some cases, the search firm's assignment will include broader human resources issues (for example, defining a position) as well as seeking candidates for a particular position.

Some firms work on both a retainer and contingency basis. Others work solely on contingency, which means the firm is paid only if it presents a candidate who is hired by the client. Because cash flow at a retained search firm is not dependent on placing a candidate, retained search firms are often regarded as more conservative about the candidates they recommend to client companies.

Some contingency assignments are exclusive—only one firm is asked to seek candidates for the opening. In other cases, more than one search firm—and possibly the employer itself—conduct simultaneous searches. In this last situation, a search consultant may feel pressured to recommend as many candidates as soon as possible, to increase the consultant's changes of being paid.

Why do employers hire search firms? For the same reason they may hire other consultants: the search firm may have special expertise in a given function or industry as well as a well-developed network of valuable contacts. When there will be significant changes in a company's management, one consultant may be able to organize a team of specialized recruiters, each seeking candidates in a different function. By using a search firm, an employer can also keep an opening confidential for a longer period. Finally, when an employer is interested in people employed by its competitors or customers, the initial contacts are often more discreetly made by a search consultant.

What makes it likely that you'll be contacted by a search consultant? Three important factors: visibility in your function or industry, a demonstrated record of accomplishments and expertise that's currently in demand. You also need to be working in—or have just recently left—a senior-level position. The larger retained search firms usually focus on positions that pay at least $100,000. Regional search consultants and firms with very specialized practices may handle professional-level and middle-management positions where some salaries are slightly less.

Helping search consultants, perhaps by referring them to candidates for an open position or providing other advice, is also likely to result in you being remembered when a search is underway.

Suppose search consultants aren't calling you. Should you be calling them? Maybe. Most retained search consultants interviewed for this book said placements seldom occurred from unsolicited resumes. Some consultants will accept unsolicited resumes, but will retain only those that they believe may be useful. Even the resumes that are filed will not result in a telephone response or an interview unless a candidate happens to match the profile developed for a current search.

If you read the following pages carefully, you'll note that some recruiters do not want—and will not respond to—"cold calls" and unsolicited resumes. Ignoring these consultants' preferences is almost guaranteed to ensure you won't be considered for any of the clients' openings—current or future. This is particularly important to remember in a market as small as Seattle's, where the employers in your industry may have long-standing relationships with just a few search consultants.

4. Retained Search Firms
The U.S.'s Largest

Retained search firms are the most prestigious of the placement profession-als. As noted in the previous chapter, these firms work on a consulting basis, usually helping a client company define its needs and outline a position as well as conducting the search for a senior management position. Retained search firms are paid whether or not the position is filled.

Executive Recruiter News, issued by Kennedy Publications (http://www.kennedypub.com), regularly ranks retained search firms by their revenues. Among the top 20 search firms on a recent ranking were the following firms with a Seattle-area presence:

Heidrick & Struggles
4 Embarcadero Center, #3570
San Francisco CA 94111
(415) 981-2854
Fax: (415) 981-0482
http://www.h-s.com
Contact: Jeff Hodge, manager
The second largest U.S. retained executive search firm, according to *Executive Recruiter News*. Maintains a general practice, but does not handle searches for positions paying less than $150,000 base. Usually at the vice president or CEO level, these jobs typically require 10-15 years experience, a B.A. and often a graduate degree. Northwest searches often involve high technology clients as well as traditional manufacturing. One Los Angeles associate telecommutes from the Seattle area, where she handles national searches for health care:

Karen Quint
(206) 230-6464
Fax: (206) 230-6468
kdq@h-s.com

Korn/Ferry International Executive Search
600 University, #3428
Seattle WA 98101
(206) 447-1834
Fax: (206) 447-9261
http://www.kornferry.com
The U.S.'s largest retained search firm. Headquartered in New York. Its Seattle office specializes in high technology. Also places general managers; handles no government or health care searches here. About half of this office's business is for local positions. Other branches also handle Seattle clients. Restricts its practice to upper level positions paying at least $100,000 base and requiring at least 10 years

experience. Scannable resumes can be mailed or faxed to the office; does not accept unsolicited e-mail.

Other large retained search firms with West Coast offices include:

A.T. Kearney Executive Search
3 Lagoon Dr., #160
Redwood City CA 94065
(415) 637-6600
(415) 637-6699
http://www.atkearney.com
Headquartered in Chicago. Handles only very high-level positions, usually those paying in excess of $100,000. The office above is the closest to Seattle.

Boyden International
275 Battery St., #420
San Francisco CA 94111
(415) 981-7900
www.boyden.com
Headquartered in New York. Ranked 19th on a recent *Executive Recruiter News* survey. Also has a Los Angeles office.

Christian & Timbers
20833 Stevens Creek Blvd., #200
Cupertino CA 95014
(408) 446-5440
Fax: (408) 446-5445
http://www.ctnet.com
Conducts national searches for positions at and above the director and vice president level, with salaries of $140,000 and greater. Several offices; this is the one closest to Seattle.

DHR International
19200 Von Karman, #500
Irvine CA 92715
(714) 622-5520
Fax: (714) 622-5521
www.lagrow.com

Egon Zehnder International
100 Spear St., #920
San Francisco CA 94105
(415) 228-5200
Fax: (415) 904-7801
www.zehnder.com
EZO-SFO-Research@ezi.net

Johnson Smith & Knisely Accord
44 Montgomery St., #3060
San Francisco CA 94104
(415) 782-2280

Kenzer Corp.
6033 W. Century Blvd., #808
Los Angeles CA 90045
(310) 417-8577
Fax: (310) 417-3083
www.kenzer.com
kenzerla@worldnet.att.net
This New York-based firm provides examples of its current searches on the web site.

Ray & Berndtson
2029 Century Park E., #1000
Los Angeles CA 90067
(310) 557-2828
Fax: (310) 277-0674
http://www.prb.com
The sixth largest retained search firm in the U.S. Headquartered in Texas. Typically places at the vice president and higher levels, in positions requiring a graduate degree and at least seven to 10 years experience and paying in excess of $90,000. The firm's web site offers an "Executive Profile Database" where you can create an online resume.

Russell Reynolds Associates
2500 Sand Hill Rd., #105
Menlo Park CA 94025-7015
(415) 233-2400
Fax: (415) 233-2499
http://www.russreyn.com
New York-based. Fourth largest U.S. retained search firm. Its 30 offices worldwide are organized across industry, rather than region, so all searches for the Seattle area do not necessarily go through the Northern California offices. However, the Menlo Park office does have a team specializing in technology. Focus: executive level positions, often requiring graduate degrees and several years of experience.

Russell Reynolds Associates
101 California St., #3140
San Francisco CA 94111-5830
(415) 352-3300
Fax: (415) 781-7690
http://www.russreyn.com

SpencerStuart
525 Market St., #3700
San Francisco CA 94105
(415) 495-4141

Ward Howell International
16255 Ventura Blvd., #400
Encino CA 91436
(818) 905-6010

Witt/Kieffer Ford Hadelman & Lloyd
2000 Powell St., #1645
Emeryville CA 94608
(510) 420-1370
Fax: (510) 420-0363
elainag@wittkieffer.com
Contact: Elaina Genser, senior vice president, Northern California
Specializes in health care and academic administrators at the director and higher levels. Ranked 12th largest by *Executive Recruiter News*. Headquartered in Illinois.

5. Executive Search Firms:
Locally Based

You're a controller or CFO, an experienced pharmaceutical sales rep, an HR director, a vice president of marketing, an attorney. You're ready for a move—up the ladder or to a different environment. You've read the ads and revived your network...but you're wondering which search firms may be seeking people like you for their client companies.

This chapter is based on hundreds of interviews in mid and late 1997 with executive recruiters. Most of the firms listed here are based in the Pacific Northwest; many have regional practices and one or two offices. The chapter concludes with the examples of those smaller firms headquartered elsewhere who have recently conducted searches in this area.

In each case, search professionals were asked about their specialties and whether they would accept unsolicited resumes and telephone calls. Those few firms that declined to provide adequate information are not included.

Now, as part of your job search, should you be contacting these consultants and placement professionals? Maybe—and in some cases, probably not. Before you fire off a stack of resumes or pick up the phone, note carefully the minimum experience in a job typically required by a particular firm's clients. Remember that although some local firms do file unsolicited resumes, such resumes seldom result in placements. (Many search consultants said they may have made such placements once in their careers.) To make yourself visible to search consultants, it may be wiser to follow some of the suggestions in *Selling Yourself to Recruiters and Employers*.

Firms are included in this chapter if they defined themselves as search consultants. Because some also handle contract or interim positions, you'll also find them listed in *Contract Employment*. Firms that fill administrative support as well as "executive" positions (which some recruiters define as those paying in excess of $30,000) will also be listed in *Employment Agencies*.

Accountants Executive Search
601 Union St., #1625
Seattle WA 98101
(206) 467-0700
Fax: (206) 467-9986
aoc@seanet.com
Contact: Randy Back, executive recruiter
A division of Accountants On Call, this office provides permanent placement in accounting and finance positions paying $30,000 or more. Accounting positions, which range from staff accountant to CFO, require an accounting degree and usually a CPA or CMA. For finance positions, which range from financial analyst to director of financial planning and analysis, you'll need a degree in finance or

accounting. What's preferred: an MBA and experience in modelling and variance analysis. To inquire about openings, call first and then have a resume prepared to mail or e-mail.

Accountants Inc.
500 108th N.E., #2350
Bellevue WA 98004
(425) 454-4111
Fax: (425) 454-4906
http://www.accountantsinc.com
bellevue@accountantsinc.com
Contact: Elizabeth Look, branch manager
Specializes in temporary (one day to one year) and permanent placement in accounting and finance. Two local offices; all fees employer-paid. Positions range from accounting clerk to CFO and finance director. Candidates should have a stable work history; a B.A. is sufficient for many positions, but you'll need a CPA for the top accounting jobs and an MBA for many finance opportunities. (Tip: you'll have a better chance at the best jobs if you have a well-prepared resume and if you can present yourself well in person.)

Accountants Inc.
1420 Fifth Ave., #1711
Seattle WA 98101
(206) 621-0111
Fax: (206) 621-0285
http://www.accountantsinc.com
mrefvem@accountantsinc.com
Contact: Mary Refvem, branch manager

Accounting Partners
500 108th Ave. N.E., #1640
Bellevue WA 98004
(425) 450-1990
Fax: (425) 450-1056
http:/www.apartner.com
Specializes in accounting and finance, doing both temporary and permanent placements. Positions range from accounting clerk to controller, from data entry to financial analyst. Most upper level accounting positions are for staff accountants; you should have an accounting degree and one to three years experience. A CPA is an excellent credential, but not as important as the appropriate experience. Such positions pay $11-$15 an hour. A financial analyst should have at least two years experience; a degree is preferred. You'll also need proficiency with a spreadsheet management program. Almost all jobs require DOS or Windows. A junior analyst might make $10-$12 an hour, a more senior person $15-$25.

Accounting Quest
101 Stewart St., #1000
Seattle WA 98101
(206) 441-5600
Fax: (206) 441-5656
gregg@accountingquest.com
Contact: Greg Gillard, office director
Specialty: temporary and permanent positions in accounting and finance for high-technology and high-growth companies between Tacoma and Everett. Also offices in Portland and Denver. Positions range from accounting clerk to accounting manager, which might pay $40,000-$50,000, and controller, which might pay $50,000-$80,000; to senior financial analysts and finance directors, which might pay $40,000-$90,000; and to MIS systems implementation jobs, which might pay $35,000-$90,000. Lower-level positions require accounting education or fast data entry and a stable work history; for all positions, you'll need good references, evidence of progressively more responsible professional growth, a can-do attitude and enthusiasm. To apply, call or submit a resume (two pages maximum). Works on a contingency basis with all fees employer-paid.

ACS & Associates
2835 82nd Ave. S.E., #201
Mercer Island WA 98040
(206) 728-8028
Fax: (206) 236-8104
ACSTEC@aol.com
Contact: Carl Smith, principal
A local executive search firm established in 1986. Usually paid on a retainer basis. Two specialties: the high tech industry, mostly for technical (e.g., project engineer) and financial positions; and the public sector, for management jobs and such staff positions as human resources. For the high tech jobs, candidates should have at least two or three years of applicable experience; a degree is preferred. For the government opportunities, you'll need five to 10 years of experience in management. How to approach: send a resume (two pages maximum) with a cover letter that describes the position you seek, your salary expectations and whether you'll relocate.

Adams & Associates
701 Fifth Ave., #3700
Seattle WA 98104
(206) 447-9200
http://www.adamsandassoc.com
Executive search: search@adamsandassoc.com
This locally owned firm has three divisions: executive search, for positions paying $55,000 and more; office support (OCD), for permanent placements in administrative support; and Adams Temporaries, for temporary and temp-to-hire placements. Typical executive search placements are for controllers, account executives, regional sales managers and marketing managers. Most require at least three to five years experience, a degree and documented success in previous positions. All fees employer paid.

Almond & Associates

P.O. Box 6124
Federal Way WA 98063-6124
(253) 952-5555; from Seattle: (206) 721-1111
Fax: (253) 952-5560
Contact: John Almond
This local firm provides executive search on a national basis for positions paying
$50,000 or more. For a position such as CFO or vice president, finance, typical
qualifications are a degree and eight or more years relevant experience. The firm
also fills administrative support positions. All fees employer-paid.

Anchor Staffing   *R*

160 N.W. Gilman Blvd., #3
Issaquah WA 98027
(425) 837-1355
Fax: (425) 837-1715
anchor_sr@msn.com
Contact: Pamela Gotham, principal
Established in 1995, this local firm provides executive search for interim and
permanent positions in sales, technology, manufacturing and accounting. Positions range from contract programmers in information systems to mid and senior
management. Candidates for executive positions should have at least two years
experience in that function. The agency also offers temporary and permanent
placement in medical and health professions and clerical and light industrial
positions. All fees are employer-paid. To apply, you can call, write or e-mail; your
resume (scannable, maximum two pages) will be filed for a year.

B & M Unlimited   *NO GOOD*

1218 Third Ave., #1518
Seattle WA 98101
(206) 223-1687
Fax: (206) 343-5555
bmunlim@aol.com
Contact: (Mr.) Lonnie Moore, president
Established in 1977, this local agency handles local government and private sector
positions, in functions ranging from administrative support to accounting and
finance (for example, CFO) to division management. All fees employer paid. If you
submit a resume, it'll be retained for six months and reviewed regularly; you'll be
contacted if the firm has a position that fits your background.

Barbara Ruhl & Associates

15 Diamond F Ranch
Bellevue WA 98004
(425) 453-7299
Fax: (425) 453-7801
Contact: Barbara Ruhl
This local search firm, founded in 1991, handles positions in mortgage, escrow and
property management. All fees employer-paid. Unsolicited resumes are accepted
if they don't exceed two pages and are scannable.

Berkana International

18907 Forest Park Dr. N.E.
Seattle WA 98155
(206) 361-1633
Fax: (206) 361-1630
http://www.headhunters.com
sonja@headhunters.com
Contact: Sonja Carson, president
Founded in 1988, this local search firm focuses on such high technology functions as software development, new media and cross-platform security. Seventy per cent of its clients are between Seattle and Portland; most work is done on retainer. Clients may be as small as start-ups (pre-IPO) or as large as Fortune 100 firms. To qualify for a typical technical position, you're likely to need a B.A. in math or physics and a master's in computer science and five or more years experience with commercial software. For a marketing position, a technical B.A. and an MBA are preferred along with experience in getting a high-quality commercial software product to market. To apply, submit a descriptive letter and/or resume via e-mail, fax or mail and then follow up with a phone call.

Black & Deering

1605 116th Ave. N.E., #211
Bellevue WA 98004
(425) 646-0905
Fax: (425) 451-0335
Contact: George Deering
Health care institutions—acute medical and surgical—are the focus of this local retained search firm, which places department managers to CEOs. Most positions do not require medical degrees, although many candidates have nursing as well as management experience. Serves Washington, Oregon, Idaho and Montana. Typical base salaries are $65,000-$115,000, with performance-based compensation packages increasingly common. If you submit a resume, it should be scannable and no more than two pages in length; it'll be retained for six months.

Business Careers

600 108th N.E., #246
Bellevue WA 98004
(425) 447-7411
Fax: (425) 447-5217
Contact: Jerry Taylor, executive recruiter
Bellevue is the headquarters for this locally-owned agency, which handles executive search from this office. Executive recruiter Jerry Taylor works on a contingency basis. Typical positions are in sales, including entry-level; management, including trainees; accounting; and technical, including entry-level engineers and tech support.

Caplan, Sally

See Sally Caplan & Associates

Career Specialists
155 108th N.E., #200
Bellevue WA 98004
(425) 455-0582
Fax: (425) 646-9738
Contact: Pamela Rolfe, principal
Established in 1969, this local retained search firm specializes in senior management, for Washington and Oregon positions requiring eight or more years experience and offering a base salary of at least $85,000. Typical positions might range from vice president, human resources to CEO.

Clevenger, Susan
see Susan Clevenger Executive Search

Construction Management Services
40 Lake Bellevue Dr., #100
Bellevue WA 98005
(425) 868-2211
Fax: (425) 868-6622
http://www.cms-seattle.com
Contact: Mark Mannon, president
Construction management professionals—estimators, superintendents, field engineers, project managers and construction managers—are the specialty of this local firm, in business since 1982. Makes permanent placements from Portland to Bellingham, from entry-level to executives. Pay range: $30,000-$100,000. Works on a contingency basis.

Cook, Kim Finch, Executive Recruiter
See Kim Finch Cook Executive Recruiter

Corbett & Associates
1215 S. Central, #204-A
Kent WA 98032
(253) 854-1906
Fax: (253) 854-1485
http://www.corbettrecruiting.com
A local firm with clients across the U.S. in medical and pharmaceutical sales, sales management and marketing. These permanent positions usually require at least two or three years outside sales experience (although occasionally someone with 18 months experience can be considered). To inquire, you can call and then fax your resume. All fees employer paid.

The Coxe Group
1218 Third Ave., #1700
Seattle WA 98101-3021
(206) 467-4040
Fax: (206) 467-4038
http://www.coxegroup.com
consultants@coxegroup.com
Founded in Philadelphia in the 1970s and moved here in 1991, this consulting firm

for architecture and engineering design offers executive search services. Most clients, however, are outside the Seattle area. Most positions require at least five or 10 years experience. If you submit a resume, it must be scannable. If you're using e-mail, a Microsoft Word document is preferred; it should be accompanied by a cover letter explaining your focus, your salary expectations and your willingness to relocate.

CRW Executive Search Consulting
11719 90th Ave. N.E.
Kirkland WA 98034
(425) 814-5373
Fax: (425) 821-1769
crwexecusearch@msn.com
A local retained search firm established in 1996 to specialize in positions in finance, accounting, tax and information systems at the vice president and higher level. Does not accept unsolicited resumes.

Cushman, Judith
See Judith Cushman & Associates

Devon James Associates
12356 Northup Way, #118
Bellevue WA 98005
(425) 885-3050
Fax: (425) 881-7168
http://www.devonjames.com
devonjames@devonjames.com
Contact: Colleen Aylward, principal
Established in 1992, this search firm specializes in executive level positions (for example, sales managers and higher) for high technology. Most positions are in the Puget Sound area and pay at least $50,000. Most require a minimum of three to five years similar experience.

Drake Personnel
520 Pike St., #1520
Seattle WA 98101
(206) 623-5552
Fax: (206) 623-7336
Contact: Ann McElroy, branch manager
A branch of a Toronto firm. Handles permanent placement of professionals and managers in such positions as operations manager, sales manager, programmer, assembly technician, controller and CEO. Most positions require at least a B.A. and three years experience in a similar job. Pay: at least $35,000. Works on a contingency basis. To apply, call and then submit a resume (two pages maximum, reverse chronological format). The dates you held each position should be clearly noted. Project managers should submit resumes listing projects, with the dates and clients for each specified. Will relocate to another downtown Seattle location by 1998.

Eber Finance Inc.
600 University St., #2400
Seattle WA 98101
(206) 343-5390
Fax: (206) 624-7579
deber@wolfenet.com
Contact: Deena Eber
A CPA herself, Deena Eber specializes in executive search for accounting and finance positions for such industries as telecommunications, software, biomedicine and biotechnology. Positions range from staff accountant and accounting manager to CFO. In finance, where positions often need an MBA, opportunities might range from analyst to director or vice president. Occasional contract opportunities; a job-share can sometimes be structured when a candidate wishes to work part-time. To have your resume added to Eber's database, submit it by mail, e-mail or fax; do not telephone. Eber works on a contingency basis.

Egan, Kathi
See Kathi Egan Associates

Executive Recruiters
P.O. Box 1766
Bellevue WA 98009
(206) 447-7404
Fax: (425) 451-8424
info@execr.com
Contact: Jerry Taylor, manager
Affiliated with Business Careers and Careers Northwest, this local firm was established in 1970. Focus: senior professional staff, in finance, human resources, sales and marketing, engineering and professional services. Also fills such high tech positions as software development, Internet and intranet development, multimedia, electronic commerce, wireless communications, telecommunications and the disk drive (media) industry. About 40 per cent of the positions filled are local. Most require a minimum of four or five years experience and provide a base salary of $70,000 or more. Fees are employer paid.

Executive Search International (ESI)
710 N.W. Juniper, #204
Issaquah WA 98027
(425) 391-2465
Fax: (425) 557-9925
esearchint@aol.com
Contact: Dave Johnson, chairman/CEO
Focus: wireless telecommunications, with positions ranging from junior technician to senior management. Most placements are for mid-management or higher positions; about half are technical. Headquartered here, this firm is a franchisor. Works on retainer or contingency basis. To add your resume to ESI's files, submit it via fax or e-mail.

Falcon Associates

9603 117th Pl. N.E.
Kirkland WA 98033
(425) 822-3342
lyler@concentric.net
Contact: Lyle Radcliffe, CEO
High technology is the focus of this search firm, which finds candidates for such positions as operations director, COO and vice presidents of sales and engineering. Most positions pay a base of at least $75,000. Local firm, but many clients are elsewhere in the country.

Feldman Associates

3002 N.E. 87th
Seattle WA 98115
(206) 527-0980
Fax: (206) 527-1312
Contact: Renee Feldman
Specialty: sales, sales management and technical (operations, engineering) management positions in the chemical, industrial products, building products, plastics and packaging industries. Positions pay $50,000-$200,000. Most require several years experience and at least a B.A., usually in mechanical, chemical, manufacturing or industrial engineering. A local firm with national clients; about 40 per cent of the searches are for local jobs. Paid on a contingency basis. Founded in 1990.

Foote, L.W.

See L. W. Foote Company

F-O-R-T-U-N-E Personnel Consultants of East King County

11661 S.E. 1st St., #202
Bellevue WA 98005
(425) 450-9665
Fax: (425) 450-0357
fortuneseattle@seanet.com
Contact: Dan Chin, president
Industry focus: heavy manufacturing, including heavy equipment, mobile equipment and materials handling. Within these industries, fills engineering (electrical, mechanical and industrial), purchasing and sales management positions at the mid-management and higher levels. Works for national clients, but all positions are here. Paid on a contingency basis. Established in 1995.

Franklin Search Group

See Medzilla/The Franklin Search Group

Gary Kokensparger & Associates

800 Bellevue Way N.E., #400
Bellevue WA 98004
(425) 637-2836
Fax: (425) 882-9590
garykandassoc@msn.com
Contact: Gary Kokensparger, principal

A local search firm that fills half of its positions here in information technology and information systems jobs ranging from programmer to director. Minimum experience: two to three years. If you'd like to be considered for the firm's database, submit a resume with a letter that indicates your ability to travel. Candidates already must have legal authority to work in the U.S. to be considered.

Gordon Kamisar Esq. National Legal Search Consultants

1509 Queen Anne Ave. N., #298
Seattle WA 98109
(425) 392-1969
Fax: (425) 557-0080
http://www.seattlesearch.com
gkamisar@sprynet.com
Contact: Gordon Kamisar, Esq., principal
Attorneys for both private practice and corporate counsel is the specialty of this local firm founded in 1990. About 90 per cent of its placements are in the Seattle area. Many positions require three to six years experience in high tech; for example, in intellectual property or securities. To contact the firm, submit a resume via fax or e-mail and follow up by mail. Works on a contingency basis.

Goto & Company

7981 168th Ave. N.E., #27
Redmond WA 98052
(425) 869-8092
Fax: (425) 881-9500
hiroshigoto@msn.com
Contact: Hiroshi Goto
Nearly all the clients for this local search firm are Japanese firms seeking staff for Northwest offices. Some positions are entry-level; others are supervisory or at the vice president level. Some candidates must be bilingual. All fees are employer paid. Resumes may be submitted by fax, mail or e-mail.

Hagel & Co.

1111 Third Ave., #2500
Seattle WA 98101
(206) 624-6674
success@hagel.net
Contact: Frank Hagel
Works on a retainer basis in Washington and Oregon in the public sector, for not-for-profits and in business, especially banking. Most searches involve positions at the director or higher level and require at least at least seven years of experience and a B.A. (with some clients preferring a graduate degree). Established in 1993. Accepts unsolicited resumes only by e-mail; retains only those resumes applicable to typical searches.

Headden & Associates

777 108th Ave. N.E., #600
Bellevue WA 98004
(425) 451-2427
Fax: (425) 646-3015
Contact: Bill Headden

Founded in 1978, this firm works on a retainer basis, filling middle to senior management positions that typically require at least eight to 10 years experience. Most positions pay $80,000-$200,000. About a quarter of the positions filled are in this area. Your resume will be kept on file if relevant to the firm's usual searches. Affiliated with The Lorenzen Group.

Healthcare Specialists
400 108th Ave. N.E., #310
Bellevue WA 98004
Fax: (425) 454-6776
Contacts:
Deni Sutherland, recruiter: (425) 454-0678
Lisa Ward, recruiter: (425) 454-9313
Founded by Kathy Evans in 1976, this sales and sales management search firm now has new owners and a new name. The focus remains the same: outside sales and sales management for the medical, dental and pharmaceutical industries. For an entry-level position, you'll need at three to five years successful experience in outside sales and a degree (some employers also require a grade point average of at least 3.0). Many candidates come from sales jobs in consumer products, business products or the cellular industry. Such positions may pay $50,000 plus a car allowance. For higher level positions, employers prefer applicable industry experience (e.g., in the cardio-vascular field) and candidates with established contacts. Works on a contingency basis.

Helstrom Turner & Associates
10900 N.E. 8th St., #900
Bellevue WA 98004
(425) 868-1617
Fax: (425) 868-5385
htaseattle@aol.com
Contact: (Ms.) Kim Villeneuve, partner
Headquartered in Los Angeles, this woman-owned search firm specializes in the retail and restaurant industries. Only about five per cent of its searches are for positions in the Seattle area. Positions range from trend manager to CEO. Most require at least 10-15 years experience. Works on retainer. Particularly interested in women candidates with senior-level experience. To contact the firm, submit a resume (two pages maximum).

Hembree Galbraith & Associates
40 Lake Bellevue, #100
Bellevue WA 98005
(425) 646-8916
In the Seattle area since 1985, this firm specializes in high technology sales and marketing jobs. Most require at least five years experience and a degree and pay $80,000 or more. Although most positions are based here, they usually require travel—often extensive travel. Does not accept unsolicited resumes.

High Tech Recruiters LLC
19125 North Creek Pkwy.
Bothell WA 98011
(425) 482-9877, (800) 644-9164
Fax: (425) 402-1948
http://www.hightechrecruiters.com
recruiters@msn.com
Contact: Lynn Launer
A local form that specializes in senior-level technical staff (for example, senior developers, testers, program managers and product managers) and executives for computer hardware and software firms. Seeks comparable experience in the same industry. Works in Washington and Oregon. A special concern: matching the culture of the company with that of the candidate. Works on a contingency basis.

Houser, Martin, Morris & Associates
P.O. Box 90015
Bellevue WA 98009
(425) 453-2700
Fax: (425) 453-8726
http://www.houser.com
Contact: Bob Holert, president
Established here in 1974; specializes in technical staff, managers and executives. Also handles executive director searches for trade associations and government agencies and attorney openings in private practices and corporations. In information systems, fills positions from PC technician and up; in human resources, from employment specialist; and in marketing and sales, from public relations specialist and account executive. Most technical positions pay at least $40,000; most sales jobs at least $45,000 and most accounting positions, $50,000-$90,000. Most require a B.A. (many a master's degree) and a minimum of three years experience. Works on both a contingency and retainer basis.

HR Services Inc.
1001 Fourth Ave., #3200
Seattle WA 98154
(206) 340-1471
Fax: (206) 340-0113
http://www.aa.net/hrservices
hrsvcs@aa.net
Contact: Victoria Cobos, president
Human resources positions (from recruiters, compensation specialist and benefits analysts to managers) on a temporary (three months or longer) and permanent basis are the specialty of this local firm established in 1988. Some part-time opportunities, both temporary and permanent. Most positions require four to seven years corporate (rather than employment agency) experience, a degree and CEBS or equivalent certification. Temporary assignments pay $14-$30 an hour, permanent positions $35,000-$75,000. All fees employer paid.

HRA Insurance Staffing

11100 N.E. 8th St., #600
Bellevue WA 98004
(425) 451-4007
Contact: Cindy Boe, managing partner
Specialty: permanent property casualty insurance positions along Puget Sound's
Interstate 5 corridor. Even entry-level candidates should have at least a year of
experience in an insurance company or brokerage. Established in 1986; locally
owned. Works on a contingency basis.

Humphrey Recruiting

P.O. Box 8067
Tacoma WA 98408
(253) 862-8806; from Bellevue: (425) 451-0330
Voice mail: (253) 474-8042
Fax: (253) 862-3689
Contact: Diann Humphrey, president
Thinking resorts, clubs, restaurants or hotels? This local firm specializes in mid-
management and higher hospitality placements (including executive chef) in
Washington, Oregon, Idaho, California and British Columbia. Positions pay a
minimum of $30,000. Works with experienced candidates; a degree or specialized
training is helpful. You'll also need a stable work history (candidates who are
currently or were until recently employed are preferred) and a record of accomplishments. For example, a candidate for an executive chef position needs to
demonstrate profitability.

Humphrey/Nelson Group

1420 Fifth Ave., #2200
Seattle WA 98101
(206) 224-2887
Fax: (206) 224-2880
Contacts: John Humphrey and Nena Nelson, principals
Established in 1997. Affiliated with Career Transition Associates, a corporate and
retail outplacement firm founded by the same principals in 1985. Specializes in
technical professionals, managers and salespeople and human resources staff,
from receptionists to vice presidents. A candidate for a software engineering or
programming job should have at least two years experience and a B.S.; technical
managers and sales reps should have at least five years experience and a minimum
of a bachelor's degree. HR manager-candidates should have at least five years
experience and a B.A. To submit your credentials, call the Seattle office for a
telephone screening.

Humphrey/Nelson Group

800 Bellevue Way, #400
Bellevue WA 98004
(425) 562-8030

Hurd Siegal & Associates
1111 Third Ave., #2880
Seattle WA 98101
(206) 622-4282
Fax: (206) 622-4058
hsiegal2@compuserve.com
Contact: Larry Siegal, principal
A local search firm established in 1991 that does about 25 per cent of its placements
in the Seattle area. Focus: senior management (directors and above) for manufacturing and distribution companies. If you submit a resume, it'll be kept on file for
a year.

Interim Search Solutions
777 108th Ave. N.E., #1200
Bellevue WA 98004
(425) 462-7004
Fax: (425) 462-0752
http://www.interim.com
jmilller@ji.com
Focus: high technology and earth and engineering sciences. Positions may range
from NT engineer and senior C++ programmer to water planner and bridge
engineer. Typical compensation: $50,000 and more. Most positions require at least
three years experience and a degree.

Jensen & Cooper
411 108th N.E., #250
Bellevue WA 98004
(425) 637-5656
Fax: (425) 637-5657
jencoop@aol.com
Contacts: Bruce Jensen and Jan Cooper, principals
A local search firm that makes 50 to 75 per cent of its placements in this area, but
also does work in Alaska and Texas. Most clients are privately owned companies,
often in emerging industries or professional services; most positions are at or
above the director level and pay $80,000 or more. If your background matches the
kind of searches the firm typically does, your resume (two pages maximum
preferred) will be filed for several months. Works on a retainer basis.

John Mason & Associates
P.O. Box 3823
Bellevue WA 98009
(425) 453-1608
Fax: (425) 883-2997
masonsail@aol.com
Contact: John Mason
Eighty per cent of this search firm's business is in the technology industry, almost
always for positions in the Seattle area. A typical position pays $65,000 and
requires five to 15 years experience; most require degrees and about 20 per cent
specify a graduate degree. They range from project or department managers to
general managers. A local firm, established in 1978. Works on contingency and
retainer basis.

Jones Consulting Group

1335 N. Northlake Way, #101
Seattle WA 98103
(206) 548-0109
Fax: (206) 545-8339
jones_search_partners@msn.com
Contact: Janet Jones, principal
Specialties: consumer packaged goods (especially wine) and construction management (both commercial and production residential), usually for positions paying at least $100,000 and requiring more than eight years experience. If your background matches the kind of searches the firm typically does, you can mail in (not fax) a resume that'll be filed for a year. Works on a retainer basis.

Judith Cushman & Associates

1125 12th Ave. N.W., #B-1A
Issaquah WA 98027
(425) 392-8660
Fax: (425) 391-9190
http://www.jc-a.com
info@jc-a.com
Contact: Judith Cushman, president
A locally owned firm that specializes in mid to senior level marketing communications including public relations and investor relations positions. National and local clients. Emphasis in high technology. Works on a retainer basis. For marketing communications professionals with fewer than five years experience, has established The Recruiting Connection.

Kathi Egan Associates

2611 N.E. 125th St., #204
Seattle WA 98125
(206) 361-4802
Contact: Kathi Egan
This search firm does not accept unsolicited resumes but will consider calls from qualified candidates. Focus: property casualty insurance, for positions that require at least three to five years experience. Works in Washington, Oregon, northern Idaho and Alaska on a contingency basis.

Kamisar, Gordon

See Gordon Kamisar Esq. National Legal Search Consultants

Key Staff LLC

600 University St., #1720
Seattle WA 98101
(206) 667-8911
Fax: (206) 667-8921
http://www.keystaff.com
keystaff@keystaff.com
Contacts:
Kay A. Terry, president
Karen P. Storey, executive vice president

Specialty: accounting and finance positions to CFO and information technology positions to CIO and vice president, some paying as much as $150,000. Serves clients from Tacoma to Everett. A local firm established in 1996. You can submit a resume by e-mail or fax. Works on a contingency basis.

Kim Finch Cook Executive Recruiter
9805 N.E. 116th St., #7345
Kirkland WA 98034
(425) 485-7490
Fax: (425) 402-3446
kfcook@ibm.net
Contact: Kim Cook, principal
Established in 1994, this local search firm specializes in finance, treasury and accounting. Work is done either on a contingency or retainer basis. Most positions require at least four years experience and pay $45,000 or more.

Kokensparger, Gary
See Gary Kokensparger & Associates

Kossuth & Associates
800 Bellevue Way, #400
Bellevue WA 98004
(425) 450-9050
Fax: (425) 450-0513
kossuth@halcyon.com
Contact: Jane Kossuth, principal
A three-person search firm specializing in software and telecommunications industry positions, both technical and general, that pay at least $60,000. Most require a minimum of five years experience and a degree. Unsolicited resumes are accepted, but you will not be interviewed unless your background matches the needs of a current client.

L. W. Foote Company
110 110th Ave. N.E., #603
Bellevue WA 98004
(425) 451-1660
Fax: (425) 451-1535
http://www.wolfenet.com/~lwfoote/
email@lwfoote.com
Contacts: Leland W. Foote and James E. Bloomer
A local firm founded in 1983. Specializes in senior executive positions paying $75,000 or more in the high technology, biotechnology and electronics industries. Many West Coast clients. Works on a retainer basis. Affiliated with the Brighton Group, a corporate outplacement firm owned by Leland Foote.

Lager, Russell A.
See Russell A. Lager & Associates

Lawrence & Associates
1200 Fifth Ave., #1927
Seattle WA 98101
(206) 621-1228
Fax: (206) 624-1214
LLandTL@aol.com
Contact: (Mr.) Terry Lawrence, principal
Works on a retainer basis. About 70 per cent of the firm's searches are for such positions as controller, CFO, vice president, finance or in treasury; none pay less than $45,000 and most pay $60,000-$80,000. Also handles operations positions, usually for vice president and higher positions paying at least $60,000, and some accounting, tax and audit management positions for service businesses. Most searches are for Puget Sound-area openings. If your credentials fit the firm's usual needs, your resume will be kept on file for a year.

The Lorenzen Group
3016 W. Blaine St.
Seattle WA 98199
(206) 285-7123
Fax: (206) 285-6917
Contact: Laurie Jones Lorenzen, principal
In business since 1988, this local search firm specializes in high technology and communications (telecommunications, multi-media and data communications). Positions may be in sales and marketing, operations, MIS or general management. Most searches are at the mid to senior management level and require five to 10 years of experience; many employers prefer graduate degrees (often an MBA). About half the searches involve local positions. To be considered for the firm's database, mail your resume (two pages maximum) with a cover letter indicating your salary requirements and your ability to relocate. Works on retainer. Affiliated with Headden & Associates.

Management Recruiters International
9725 S.E. 36th, #312
Mercer Island WA 98040
(206) 232-0204
http://www.mrinet.com
mercer!@mrinet.com
Contact: Jim Dykeman, president
A franchise, this firm specializes in placements in the electrical connector, Internet software, sports apparel and pharmaceutical and nutrition industries. Level: mid to senior management, including design engineers, sales reps and sales managers, shoe designers and scientists. Salaries range from $45,000 to $150,000. About 10 per cent of the positions are local. Works on a contingency basis.

Management Recruiters International
2510 Fairview Ave. E.
Seattle WA 98102
(206) 328-0936
Fax: (206) 328-3256
http://www.mrinet.com
seattle!jrg@mrinet.com
Contact: Dan Jilka, manager
This office specializes in high technology (including aerospace and computer hardware and software) and biotechnology, with openings typically in sales and marketing and industrial control. Candidates should have five to seven years work experience (preferably in no more than two or three jobs), documented accomplishments and a degree (a sales or marketing job may also require an MBA). You should also be realistic regarding salary and relocation. Forty per cent of the placements are local. Works on a contingency basis.

Management Recruiters International
10900 N.E. Fourth St., #1450
Bellevue WA 98004
(425) 462-5104
Fax: (425) 462-1614
http://www.mrinet.com
Contact: Isaac Menda, manager
Focus: attorneys and paralegals for the securities industry. Works on a contingency basis.

Management Recruiters of Lynnwood
19109 36th W., #100
Lynnwood WA 98036
(425) 778-1212
Fax: (425) 778-7840
lynwood!bud@mrinet.com
Contact: Bud Naff, general manager
This franchise, established in 1988, specializes in permanent placements in environmental consulting and engineering, construction (for example, estimators and construction managers), civil engineering design (for example, airports, tunnels, wastewater facilities) and diagnostic imaging in health care (both hands-on professionals and managers in CAD, CT, MRI and ultrasound). Salary range: $30,000 and above. Works on a contingency basis.

Management Recruiters of Tacoma
2709 Jahn Ave. N.W.
Gig Harbor WA 98335
(253) 858-9991, (800) 863-1872
Fax: (253) 858-5140
Contact: Dennis Johnson, manager
This franchise specializes in permanent placements in medicine (doctors, nurses and therapists), health care management (usually requires a degree and at least five to 10 years of managemet experience), high technology (including software developers and project managers) and accounting and finance (controller and more senior positions). Most placements pay $50,000 or more. All fees employer paid.

Mason, John
See John Mason & Associates

McIntire & Carr
P.O. Box 1176
Issaquah WA 98027
(425) 391-9320
Fax:(425) 557-7943
mlm@halcyon.com
Contact: Merlin McIntire
Focus: sales and sales management and product management of such products as
medical and industrial equipment, pharmaceuticals, software, office products,
printing and telecommunications. Seventy-five per cent of the jobs are in Seattle
or Portland. Candidates should have at least two to five years documented success
in outside sales and a degree; for junior positions in pharmaceuticals, some
employers even require a certain grade point average. Pay: $30,000-$65,000 plus
incentive. All fees employer paid.

McKain Consulting
600 First Ave., #617
Seattle WA 98104
(206) 749-0694
Fax:(206) 749-0695
bmckain@juno.com
Contact: Brian McKain, principal
Focus: permanent positions (senior professionals and mid to senior management)
in consulting engineering and environmental consulting. Most pay at least $60,000.
Only about 15 per cent of the placements are local. Works on a retainer basis. A
local firm established in 1992.

Medic-Focus
2121 Westlake Ave. N., #401
Seattle WA 98109-2448
(206) 285-6955
Fax: (206) 285-3425
eboisen@aol.com
Contact: Elliott G. Boisen, M.D.
Since 1994, this local search firm has placed doctors in patient care and management positions, administrators, nurse practitioners and physician assistants. Most
placements are local. All fees employer paid.

Medzilla/The Franklin Search Group
14522 54th Pl. W.
Edmonds WA 98020
(425) 742-4292
Fax:(425) 742-2172
http://www.medzilla.com
info@medzilla.com
Contact: Frank Heasley
Clinical research, regulatory affairs, fermentation and data management are the

areas where this search firm needed candidates most in late 1997. Specializing in high technology, health care and biotechnology, usually on a permanent basis, it places physicians, post-docs, programmers, research associates, managers and vice presidents. Jobs require at least a B.A. (in many cases, a graduate degree) and may start as low as $35,000. Most pay $50,000 or more. Many require relocation. Works on a retainer and contingency basis.

Meyer Enterprises Counselors & Consultants
3428 85th Dr. S.E.
Everett WA 98205
(425) 335-0900
Fax: (425) 334-9192
whatnow@halcyon.com
Contact: Chaz Meyer
Most of this firm's local business is in electrical and mechanical engineering positions; most require five or more years experience and pay $35,000-$85,000. The firm also places insurance professionals and managers, but usually in California. Local firm, established in 1987. All fees employer paid.

Miller & Miller Executive Search
P.O. Box 3088
Kirkland WA 98083
(425) 827-9194
Fax: (425) 822-3145
Focus: management and occasional clinical positions (for example, discovery research) in biotechnology and biomedicine. Locally owned; founded in 1989.

Minzel & Associates
1191 Second Ave., #1900
Seattle WA 98101
(206) 689-8526
Fax: (206) 628-9506
m-and-a@msn.com
Contact: Jeff Minzel
Provides attorneys and paralegals on a temporary and temp-to-hire basis to government agencies, law firms and corporations. To apply, fax your resume; if your background meets the firm's current needs, you'll be interviewed.

Moore Recruiting Group
6947 Coal Creek Pkwy S.E., #266
Newcastle WA 98056
(425) 369-7208
Fax: (425) 271-6436
mrg@halcyon.com
Contact: Bob Moore
A local search firm specializing in insurance, including adjusters and sales and marketing positions, and high technology, including MIS staff, programmers, software developers, systems administrators and sales and marketing positions. At a minimum, candidates need a B.A. and three to five years experience. Works on a contingency basis.

Moss & Co.
12145 Arrow Point Loop N.E.
Bainbridge Island WA 98110
(206) 842-4035
Contact: Barbara Moss
Real estate development and construction, including such positions as property manager, geotechnical engineer and contractor, are the focus of this local firm, which is paid on an hourly basis by employers. Most of the placements are local; most require at least five years experience and a degree. If your background matches the firm's usual requirements, your resume will be kept on file. Founded in 1989.

The Munro Organization
209 Parkplace, #209-G
Kirkland WA 98033
(425) 822-5700
Fax: (425) 822-5780
http://www.jobbrowser.com
sgold@serv.net
Contact: Steve Gold, manager
Headquartered in California, this firm established a Puget Sound office in 1992. Focus: high technology and information technology. About 40 to 50 per cent of the opportunities are here. Candidates should have at least two years experience; a degree is helpful.

N.G. Hayes Co.
P.O. Box 184
Medina WA 98039
(425) 453-3057
Fax: (425) 453-1313
nghayes@aol.com
Specialty: computer industry positions, ranging from technical to sales and marketing to management, from junior programmers with a couple of years experience to CEO. Most clients are between Tacoma and Everett. Established in 1991. Works on a contingency basis.

Nelson, Coulson & Associates
14450 N.E. 29th Pl., #115
Bellevue WA 98007
(425) 883-6612
Fax: (425) 883-6916
http://www.ncainc.com
denise@ncainc.com
Contact: Denise Buettgenbach, manager
A branch of a Denver firm. Focus: high technology, including aerospace engineers, electronic technicians, administrative assistants and customer service staff. Places on a temporary (two or three months or longer), contract (six months to several years) and permanent basis. Typical pay: an aerospace engineer with five to 10 years experience and a degree might make $35 an hour on contract. Works on a contingency basis.

Nesiya Inc.
2802 E. Madison St., #180
Seattle WA 98112
(206) 322-6400
Fax: (206) 322-6300
nesiyainc@aol.com
Contact: Connie R. Kanter
Focus: business positions (accounting and finance, sales and marketing, information systems and operations) in such high technology industries as medical devices, telecommunications, electronics and software. No engineering positions. Places senior professionals, managers and directors with a minimum of five to 10 years experience. Typical salary: $70,000 plus base. Most placements are in Seattle. To have your credentials considered for Nesiya's database, fax or mail in a resume (one or two pages). Candidates are more easily placed if they have experience at well-respected local firms and MBAs from top schools. Works on a contingency basis.

Northwest Legal Search
2701 N.W. Vaughn St., #450
Portland OR 97210
(503) 224-9601
Fax: (503) 224-8275
http://www.nwlegalsearch.com
greenll@aol.com
Contact: Linda Green, president
Established in 1987, this regional firm handles permanent positions for attorneys, both in private practice and corporations. Many in-house jobs are for high technology attorneys. Most candidates must have at least two years experience in practice and have graduated in the top quarter of their law school class. Academic credentials are most important for junior positions. All fees employer paid.

Northwest Professional Management Services Inc.
P.O. Box 99541
Seattle WA 98199
(206) 718-2727
Fax: (206) 284-4083
http://www.nwproman.com
phil@nwproman.com
Contact: Phil Hasenkamp
Specialty: computer technology, including programmers, software engineers, project managers, vice presidents of engineering, CIOs and occasional sales and marketing jobs. Most jobs are in the Seattle area and pay $45,000 or more. Most require at least two or three years experience. To have your credentials considered for the firm's files, submit a resume (reverse chronological format) and a minimum of three professional references. Works on a contingency and retainer basis.

The Oldani Group
188 106th Ave. N.E., #420
Bellevue WA 98004
(425) 451-3938
Fax: (425) 453-6786
http://www.theoldanigroup.com
searches@theoldanigroup.com
Contact: Jerry Oldani, principal
A local search firm specializing in executive level public sector positions (directors and above for ports and counties, typically paying at least $60,000) and, effective spring, 1998, on executive level private sector jobs. Works on a retainer basis.

Parfitt Recruiting & Consulting
P.O. Box 1932
Bellevue WA 98009
(425) 636-6300
Fax: (425) 643-6411
http://www.prcsearch.com
prc@prcsearch.com
Contact: Jan Parfitt, vice president
This local search firm, established in 1987, specializes in information technology and information systems, filling senior positions that pay from $40,000. Both contract and permanent placements. Works both on contingency and retainer basis. Affiliated with:

Parfitt, Casey & Smith
P.O. Box 1932
Bellevue WA 98009
(425) 636-6300
Fax: (425) 643-6411
http://www.prcsearch.com
prc@prcsearch.com
Established in 1997. Focus: accounting and financial management, sales and marketing management and such manufacturing positions as purchasing, production control, operations and quality control. Most positions require at least five to 10 years experience; occasionally a financial position can be filled by a CPA with less experience. Usual compensation range: $50,000-$150,000. To have your credentials considered for the firm's files, fax, mail or e-mail your resume. All fees employer paid.

Passage & Associates
1001 Fourth Ave., #3200
Seattle WA 98154
(206) 622-3330
Contact: Jim Passage, principal
Focus: middle and senior management, usually directors and higher, in positions requiring at least 10 years experience and paying $50,000 or more. Most of the firm's placements are local. Established in 1978.

Pilon Management Co.
1809 Seventh Ave., 10th floor
Seattle WA 98101
(206) 682-6465
Fax: (206) 682-6468
pilonmgt@jetcity.com
Contact: Chuck Pilon, president
A local firm established in the late 1970s. Specializes in experienced professionals, middle and senior management, for positions paying at least $30,000-$40,000. Appropriate resumes are kept on file for years. Most clients are West Coast. Works on a contingency basis.

Power Conversion International
120 W. Dayton, #B-6
Edmonds WA 98020
(425) 771-3373
Fax: (425) 771-3204
Contact: Gary Carter, principal
Headquartered here since 1989, but makes only about five per cent of its placements in this area. Focus: a wide range of functions within the power supply industry. Typical opportunities require at least four to seven years experience; only occasional entry-level positions. Fees are employer paid.

Premiere Search
25025 S.E. Klahanie Blvd., #G-205
Issaquah WA 98029
(425) 313-5099
Fax: (425) 557-3778
premiersearch@prostar.com
Contact: Richard Hugill, president
Focus: corporate franchise management positions, including operations and franchise sales. Most clients are national. Most positions require five to 10 years experience in a functional specialty or in franchising. Typical base compensation: $50,000-$70,000 in sales positions, $60,000-$80,000 in operations. Works on a contingency basis.

The Pringle Company
One S.W. Columbia, #1050
Portland OR 97258
(503) 221-0048
Fax: (503) 223-9623
tpc@pringleco.com
Works on a retained basis to fill senior management positions, often in the Pacific Northwest.

PRN MedSearch
209 E. 4th Ave., #204
Olympia WA 98501
(360) 754-4423
Fax: (360) 754-4426
http://www.halycon.com/prnmed/
prnmed@halcyon.com
Contact: Al Todak, medical recruiter
Focus: medical professionals (for example, doctors) and executives. Because Washington is a "buyers' market" for doctors, most of this firm's placements are outside the area. Works on a contingency basis.

Pro-Active Consultants
9509 Holly Dr.
Everett WA 98204
(425) 513-9200
Fax: (425) 348-9715
proactivec@aol.com
Contact: Kent Brown, president
Focus: telecommunications, both wireless and cellular, and engineering. Candidates should have at least five years industry experience; a degree is preferred. Works on contingency. To submit your credentials, call or e-mail a note first.

Pursuant Legal Consultants Attorney Placement
P.O. Box 2347
Seattle WA 98119
(206) 682-2599
Contact: Allen G. Norman, principal
Founded in New York in 1984 and relocated here in 1996, this search firm places attorneys in law firms (about a third of the firm's business) and in corporations. At least half of the firm's clients are in Seattle and Portland. Most opportunities require two to seven years experience and admission to the appropriate state's bar. Depending on current trends, may seek candidates with experience in environmental law, intellectual property or tax. To submit your credentials, mail in a cover letter that describes your background and goals along with a resume (two pages maximum). Candidates who match the firm's usual needs will be contacted. Most work is on a retainer basis.

R.A. Ward & Associates
203 Bellevue Way N.E., #492
Bellevue WA 98004
(800) 639-8127
Fax: (206) 727-5194
http://www.raward.com
info@raward.com
A search firm that specializes in health care and information technology. Seldom has searches in the Seattle area. Works on a contingency basis.

The Recruiting Connection R

1125 12th Ave. N.W., #B-1A
Issaquah WA 98027
(425) 392-8660
Fax: (425) 391-9190
http://www.jc-a.com
info@jc-a.com
Affiliated with Judith Cushman & Associates. Provides an employer-paid placement service for more junior marketing communications professionals (including public relations and investor relations), typically those with fewer than five years experience. Typical positions pay less than $55,000. See web site for submission information.

Resource Management Services R

1501 Fourth Ave., #450
Seattle WA 98101
(206) 223-8991
Fax: (206) 223-8227
resourcemgt@msn.com
Contact: Suzanne Coleman, executive administrator
Affiliated with Parker Services. Places technical professionals and managers (including web site designers, network administrators and content developers) on an interim and permanent basis in such service organizations as health care, retail, financial services and hospitality. Also places nontechnical managers in high tech companies in such jobs as finance (including controllers and financial analysts), human resources and marketing and communications (including advertising managers and sales representatives). Most positions require a degree and at least five years experience. Candidates should have have word processing, database management, spreadsheet management and Internet expertise. Salary range: $35,000-$85,000. All fees employer paid.

Richards Williams & Associates

(425) 672-3260
Fax: (425) 334-9065
rwa@seanet.com
Focus: human resources management jobs for Silicon Valley clients. Only about five per cent of the firm's searches are for jobs in Washington and Oregon. Most require three to five years experience and pay $65,000-$130,000. Address withheld upon request.

Robert Half International

601 Union St., #4300
Seattle WA 98101
(206) 749-0960
Fax: (206) 749-9243
http://www.roberthalf.com
seattle@roberthalf.com
Focus: permanent placements in MIS, accounting and finance, including such positions as bookkeeper, tax manager, CIO and CFO. Prefers candidates to have at least two years of experience. All fees employer paid.

Rod Asher & Associates
411 108th Ave. N.E., #2050
Bellevue WA 98004
(425) 646-1030
Fax: (425) 646-9141
rod@asher.com
Contact: Rod Asher
Focus: positions in the high tech industry, including software engineers and
marketing management. Most clients are in Silicon Valley.

Roth Young Executive Search of Seattle
305 111th Ave. N.E.
Bellevue WA 98004
(425) 455-2141
Fax: (425) 455-0067
Contact: Dave Salzberg, president
A licensee of a national firm; opened its office here in 1967. Does 50 per cent of
its searches for Washington, Oregon and Alaska jobs. Works on both retainer and
contingency. Focus: mid-management and higher positions in manufacturing, food
processing, the beverage and juice industries and hospitality. May also place sales
and marketing staff, from sales reps to vice presidents, in food, consumer products,
industrial, telecommunications and high tech industries.

RSA International
5200 Southcenter Blvd., #25
Seattle WA 98188
(206) 244-0554
Fax: (206) 243-3795
http://www.rsa-intl.com
rsa@rsa-intl.com
Contact: (Ms.) Sandy Antezana
Focus: information technology jobs in the Seattle area. Most (90 per cent) are
permanent. The ideal candidate has a degree in computer science and two to three
years programming language experience. Most openings pay $40,000 or more.
Works on a contingency basis.

Ruhl, Barbara
See Barbara Ruhl & Associates

Russell A. Lager & Associates
P.O. Box 60111
Seattle WA 98160
(206) 448-2616
Contact: Russell A. Lager, principal
A local firm that conducts searches in the western U.S. About 65 per cent of its
searches are for Seattle-area positions. Established in 1981. Focus: sales and
marketing positions in consumer packaged goods and food service (sales to
restaurants and institutions). Prefers candidates with at least five years experience
in consumer packaged goods. Typical base compensation: $48,000-$80,000.

Sally Caplan & Associates
1420 N.W. Gilman Blvd., #2292
Issaquah WA 98027
(425) 557-0015
Fax: (425) 557-0017
scaplan@nwlink.com
Contact: Sally Caplan, principal
Specialty: management jobs (sales, marketing, finance, accounting and general management but no programming and no human resources) in high tech and software companies. About a quarter of the firm's placements are local. Candidates should have a minimum of three to five years experience in their respective functions. Resumes (two pages maximum) can be sent in via fax or mail. A local firm, established in 1996. Works on a contingency basis.

Schoos, Susan
See Susan Schoos & Associates

SearchWest R
2104 Fourth Ave., #2120
Seattle WA 98121
(206) 728-4084
Fax: (206) 728-4087
http://www.seattle2000.com/searchwest
search@interserv.com
Contact: Bob Clark, managing director
A local firm established in 1994. Handles such high technology industry functions as product development (both software and hardware) and manufacturing and distribution. Most searches are in Washington, Oregon and Idaho. Most require a technical background and several years experience; most pay at least $50,000. Fees are employer paid.

Sheridan Company
603 Stewart St., #405
Seattle WA 98101
(206) 682-3773
Fax: (206) 682-8466
Contact: Thomas Jobe, consultant
Focus: financial services, including commercial banking, credit, international banking, international trade and sales and marketing of financial services. About 60 per cent of the positions are here, about 20 per cent in Portland. Most positions require at least two to three years of related experience and a degree in business, finance, accounting or international business. For international banking or trade, bilingual candidates (Japanese or Chinese) are more easily placed . Locally owned. Most work is on a contingency basis. Resumes (two pages maximum) can be mailed or faxed.

Strain Personnel Specialists
801 Pine St., #1900
Seattle WA 98101
(206) 382-1588
Fax: (206) 622-1572
joestrain@msn.com
Contact: Joe Strain, principal
Founded in 1983, this local firm specializes in technical positions (software developers, telephony computer integrators, testers and web developers) at the middle and senior professional level as well as marketing, finance and other business positions, usually at a senior management level, for emerging industries. Most technical positions require two or more years experience; managerial positions require several years experience. Most positions pay at least $50,000. Works on a retainer basis.

Strategic Resources Group
1697 116th Ave. N.E., #104
Bellevue WA 98004
(425) 688-1151
Fax: (425) 688-1272
http://www.strategicresources.com
info@strategicresources.com
Contact: Philip Kagan, president
Organized in 1990, this is a boutique of separate recruiters operating together. Each has different specialties: animal health and nutrition and food sciences, animal health sales and marketing; advertising; environmental engineering; apparel manufacturing and design; senior finance executives; ethnic marketing; and corporate security. Many of the searches are conducted for positions outside this area. Most jobs require at least three to five years experience and, for the sciences, often a graduate degree. Some engineering jobs require a P.E. Most pay a minimum of $50,000. Resumes can be submitted by mail, fax or e-mail; those that match the firm's needs are permanently filed on CD-ROM. Works primarily on a contingency basis.

Susan Clevenger Executive Search
2535 152nd Ave. N.E., #A
Redmond WA 98052
(425) 885-7666
Fax: (425) 869-9378
Contact: Susan Clevenger, principal
Focus: mid-range professionals and senior managers in such fields as geotechnical, property management, finance, insurance, sales and professional services. No high tech jobs or clients. Most searches involve jobs requiring at least five years experience and paying a base of at least $75,000. Candidates can mail resumes (two pages maximum) and cover letters indicating salary requirements and willingness to relocate. All fees employer paid on an hourly, contingency or retainer basis.

Susan Schoos & Associates

120 Lakeside Ave., #330
Seattle WA 98122
(206) 324-4942
Fax: (206) 328-8454
sschoos@nwlink.com
Contact: Susan Schoos
Focus: engineering, especially aviation electronics and computer hardware, and manufacturing of computer components. Most positions require a minimum of five years experience and pay $35,000-$100,000. About half of the searches are for Seattle-area jobs. Resumes are accepted by fax, but you will be called for more information only if your background matches the firm's current needs. Local firm established in the early 1990s. All fees employer paid.

Sussman & Associates

704 228th Ave. N.E., #445
Redmond WA 98053
(425) 868-8775
Fax: (425) 868-1379
sussman425@aol.com
Contact: Lori Sussman, principal
Handles senior positions (vice presidents of marketing and operations, CEOs) in satellite and space communications firms. A local company established in 1990.

Svei Hagel & Co.

P.O. Box 16484
Seattle WA 98116
(206) 935-9630
Only about 20 per cent of this firm's work is done in the Puget Sound area, in such industries as transportation and utilities, both public and private sector. Most searches require candidates with at least seven to 10 years of experience and a bachelor's degree. Most positions are at the director or higher level. Established in 1987. Does not accept unsolicited resumes.

Synergy Solutions

P.O. Box 28328
Bellingham WA 98228-0328
(360) 988-2066
Fax: (360) 988-0316
http://www.becksolutions.com
synergy@becksolutions.com
Contact: Larry Beck, president
Focus: high technology positions in programming, hardware design engineering, purchasing and management. Works on a contingency basis.

T. M. Campbell Co.
1111 Third Ave., #2500
Seattle WA 98101
(206) 583-8355
Fax: (206) 780-1705
tmcampbell@msn.com
Contact: (Ms.) Terri Campbell, principal
A local search firm established in 1992. Focus: high technology, including project managers responsible for systems implementation to chief technical officers (CTOs). Also handles searches for government, including CTOs and human resource and finance finance directors, and for public accounting firms (usually in tax or audit). Candidates often need a technical undergraduate degree and an MBA. Most positions pay at least $60,000 and are at the director or higher level. Most work is done on a retainer basis. Unsolicited calls are not welcome and unsolicited resumes will not be acknowledged unless the firm has an appropriate opening to discuss with you. However, appropriate resumes will be kept on file for six months.

The Thomas Co.
5434 S.E. 167th Pl.
Renton WA 98058
(425) 255-7637
Contact: Thomas Yankowski, executive director
Health care management (rather than clinical) and insurance positions are the specialty of this local search firm established in 1979. Positions pay at least $40,000. About a quarter of the opportunities are local. If your experience matches the firm's focus, you can mail in a resume. Those relevant to typical searches will be kept on file. All fees employer paid.

Thomas & Associates
3221 26th Ave. W.
Seattle WA 98199
(206) 283-9246
jthomas@aol.com
Contact: Jim Thomas, principal
Specialty: both clinical (doctors and nurses, for example) and management (including human resources and operations directors and CFOs) staff for health care providers (hospitals and medical groups) in several Northwestern states (including Alaska). About 30 per cent of the opportunities are in the Seattle area. Most business-side positions require five to 10 years experience and a graduate degree. How many opportunities locally are there for doctors? Depends on the specialty. Compensation? For a family practitioner, positions typically pay $100,000 or more. A local firm established in 1988.

Thompson and Associates Inc.
2448 76th Ave. S.E., #212
Mercer Island WA 98040
(206) 236-0153
Fax: (206) 236-2262
http://www.jobsnorthwest.com
neal@jobsnorthwest.com
Contact: Neal Thompson, president

Places technical people in high technology, manufacturing and service organizations in western Washington on a contract and permanent basis. Most positions require at least two years experience in the kind of job you seek. Established in 1981. Works on a contingency basis.

Thomson, Sponar & Adams (TSA, Inc.)
10116 36th Ave. Ct. S.W., #200
Lakewood WA 98499
(253) 588-1216
Fax: (253) 588-2528
http://www.aaa-mall.com/tsa/
tsa@frugal.com
Contact: Frank Adams, president
Specialty: technical professionals and managers (to CEOs) for start-ups as well as large firms in such fields as high energy physics, applied superconductivity, gas and communications, materials, computer hardware and software. At press time, the firm's searches included chemical, mechanical and cryogenics engineers, with such positions requiring either a B.S. and at least five years experience or a graduate degree and two to five years experience. All fees employer paid.

TRIAD Group
12505 Bellevue-Redmond Rd., #208
Bellevue WA 98005
(425) 454-0282
Fax: (425) 454-5784
triad@triadgrp.com
Established in 1984. Locally owned. Focus: high technology, both permanent and contract, including programming managers, web producers, technical sales representatives, product support and marketing sales support. Most positions require at least two years of experience; good technical and customer service skills are a plus. Resumes should be e-mailed; if mailed, they must be in scannable format.

Tully/Woodmansee
524 Sixth Ave. W., #210
Seattle WA 98119
(206) 285-9500
Fax: (206) 285-9299
Contact: Mary Beth Barbour, principal
One of six branches of a Florida firm; open here since 1995. Works on a retainer basis on senior management positions in retail, banking, professional services, medical devices and hospitals and high technology. At least half of this office's searches are for West Coast positions. Most positions require a minimum of three to five years experience; most pay at least $70,000. To submit your credentials, you can mail or fax a resume (with compensation levels indicated for each job).

Visionaries Sports & Entertainment Corp.
114 1/2 1st Ave. S.
Seattle WA 98104
(206) 224-9313
Fax: (206) 224-9315
newpicasso@aol.com
Contact: Rick Edwards, CEO
A local firm established in the early 1990s. Focus: experienced professionals and managers (including designers and product development and marketing staff) for sports gear manufacturers and entertainment firms. Most positions require five to 10 years experience. All fees employer paid.

Volt Executive Search
22232 17th Ave. S.E., #308
Bothell WA 98021
(425) 806-1900
Fax: (425) 806-1920
Contact: Jan Weaver
Headquartered in Orange, Calif., Volt has several divisions in the Seattle area. This is a new division that expects to handle positions at and above the vice president level. At press time, sharing space with Volt Engineering and Technical Services.

Waldron & Company
101 Stewart St., #1200
Seattle WA 98101
(206) 441-4144
Fax: (206) 441-5213
Contact: Tom Waldron, president
Handles management positions in the public sector and nonprofits. Most searches involve positions requiring at least five years experience. Affiliated with an interim placement firm, Waldron Resources, and a career search assistance firm.

Executive Search Services
Washington State Department of Personnel
600 S. Franklin
P.O. Box 47530
Olympia WA 98504-7530
(360) 664-0394
Fax: (360) 586-1369
http://www.wa.gov/DOP/employ.html
Since 1992 has served as the state's in-house executive recruiter, identifying candidates for positions as directors, deputy directors and assistant directors. Also conducts searches for city and county agencies. It is the U.S.'s only state-operated search agency. Most positions pay $50,000-$100,000. In late 1997, for example, was seeking candidates for such positions as state arts commission executive director ($55,000), state prison administrator ($60,000-$70,000), and head of Fire Protective Services ($73,500). Does not encourage unsolicited resumes.

Washington Management Service
Washington State Department of Personnel
521 Capitol Way S.
Box 47500
(360) 753-2303
Jobline: (360) 753-5368
Skills bank: (360) 753-2302
http://www.wa.gov/DOP/lib/general/wms.text
Established in 1994 to help individual agencies fill mid-management positions.
Operates a clearinghouse for state agencies seeking managers, state employees
considering job changes and private-sector managers considering government
service. Covers 3,500 positions. The web site lists departments that have five or
more WMS jobs and encourages candidates to contact these agencies directly.

Washington Firm Ltd.
2 Nickerson, Courtyard Suite
Seattle WA 98109
(206) 284-4800
Fax: (206) 270-0410
http://www.wafirm.com
resumes1@wafirm.com
Contact: Al Battson, principal
This local firm has three divisions. One unit works on a retainer basis to place
senior managers (usually requiring at least 10 years experience). A second group
provides human resources staff on a project basis. A third unit uses full-time
employees and an occasional contract employee in high tech firms to handle
information systems, information technology, engineering, software and telecommunications projects. Established in 1981. All fees employer paid.

Williams Recruiting
16336 N.E. 81st
Redmond WA 98052
(425) 869-7775
Fax: (425) 869-1849
Contact: Gail Williams, principal
A local search firm that conducts national searches for clients in biomedicine and
biotechnology, from researchers to sales and marketing executives to CEOs.
Established in 1982.

WinSearch
900 Washington St., #800
Vancouver WA 98660
(360) 906-1983; from Seattle: (206) 343-0222; toll-free: (888) 906-1983
Fax: (206) 343-2010
drbart@nwrain.com
Contact: David Bartels,principal
Despite its location, this western Washington firm places all of its candidates in the
Seattle area. Focus: high technology, including Internet development, software
and information systems. Positions include software architects and developers,

programmers and test engineers. Qualifications: at least two years of relevant experience. To submit your credentials, call or e-mail a resume. Works on a contingency basis.

Several firms headquartered elsewhere in the U.S. conduct national searches on behalf of clients in the Puget Sound area. Examples include:

Bornholdt Shivas & Friends
400 E. 87th St.
New York NY 10128-6533
(212) 557-5252
Fax: (212) 557-5704
http://members.aol/bsandf
bsandf@aol.com
Contact: John Bornholdt, president
This retained search firm works nationally, making both contract and permanent placements on the executive level. In late 1997, the firm's web site listed two Seattle-area positions, both paying about $100,000. One for a marketing director required a MBA and at least seven years experience; the other, for a president/ CEO, sought an MBA with at least 15 years of general management experience.

ERS, Inc.
150 Green Rd.
Alpharetta GA 30201
(770) 410-1858
Fax: (770) 410-0213
http://www.allhitech.com
ers@mindspring.com
Contact: Randy Shute
Occasional clients in the Puget Sound area, usually in such high tech fields as biotechnology, biomedicine, software and aerospace.

Ferneborg & Associates
1450 Fashion Island Blvd.
San Mateo CA 94404
(415) 577-0100
Fax: (415) 557-0122
john@execsearch.com
Contact: John Ferneborg
Specializes in technology and communications. Occasional Northwest opportunities.

Michael Shirley & Associates, Inc.
7300 W. 110th St., #230
Overland Park KS 66210
(913) 491-0240
Fax: (913) 491-6246
msassociates@earthlink.net
Occasional clients in the Seattle area.

6. Contract Employment

What's contract employment? Although some employers consider "temporary" and "contract" equivalent, contract employees are often highly creative or technical professionals working on long-term projects. In this market, that typically mean writers, designers and software developers. However, many firms have interim or long-term temporary assignments for senior-level professionals and managers. Two examples: personnel recruiters and controllers. This chapter includes placement professionals who handle all such positions.

Because many of the firms listed here also make permanent placements, they may also be listed in *Executive Search Firms: Locally Based* and *Employment Agencies.*

1-800-NETWORK
520 Pike St., #1345
Seattle WA 98101
(800) NETWORK
Fax: (206) 467-8469
http://www.1800network.com
resume@1800network.com
Contact: Tom Linde, market manager
A division of MacTemps, which has offices across the U.S., this agency places networking professionals on a contract and permanent basis. You'll need at least a year or two of hands-on experience; a degree is preferred, but not required for all positions. In late 1997, pay ranged from $15 to $50 an hour. For more information about opportunities, see the postings on the web site. To apply, follow the instructions on the web site or e-mail a resume as an attachment to your cover letter, which should indicate your availability, the type of work you'd like to do and the pay rate you expect. All fees are employer paid.

Able & Associates
2314 E. Union, #204
Seattle WA 98122
(206) 860-0019
Fax: (206) 860-1390
Contact: Joyce Jones, office manager
This locally-owned employment agency offers temporary and permanent placement in technical (including civil, chemical and software engineering, technical writing and free-lance writing), clerical and light industrial jobs. You can register at either the Seattle or Tacoma office. Candidates should have a stable work history (a minimum of one to three years preferred) and, especially for clerical positions, expertise with such software programs as Microsoft Office, Quicken, QuickBooks and Peachtree accounting. (Tip: When you go to register, dress as you would for an interview.)

Accountants Inc.
500 108th N.E., #2350
Bellevue WA 98004
(425) 454-4111
Fax: (425) 454-4906
http://www.accountsinc.com
bellevue@accountantsinc.com
Contact: Elizabeth Look, branch manager
Specializes in temporary (one day to one year) and permanent placement in accounting and finance. Two local offices; all fees employer paid. Positions range from accounting clerk to CFO and finance director. Candidates should have a stable work history; a B.A. is sufficient for many positions, but you'll need a CPA for the top accounting jobs and an MBA for many finance opportunities. (Tip: you'll have a better chance at the best jobs if you have a well-prepared resume and if you can present yourself well in person.)

Accountants Inc.
1420 Fifth Ave., #1711
Seattle WA 98101
(206) 621-0111
Fax: (206) 621-0285
http://www.accountantsinc.com
mrefvem@accountantsinc.com
Contact: Mary Refvem, branch manager

Accountants Northwest
520 Pike St., #2605
Seattle WA 98101
(206) 269-1133
Fax: (206) 441-6344
http://www.ntss.com
Part of Northwest Temporary Services, a local firm. Offers temporary, temporary-to-hire and permanent placement in accounting positions ranging from clerks to accounts receivable to controller.

Accountants On Call
601 Union St., #1625
Seattle WA 98101
(206) 467-0700
Fax: (206) 467-9986
http://www.aocnet.com
Affiliated with Accountants Executive Search. Handles temporary, temp-to-hire and permanent placements in accounting and finance jobs paying less than $30,000. In late 1997, estimated that a staff accountant working on a temporary basis could make $12.50-$15 an hour, a financial analyst $12-$16 and an experienced controller with CPA $18-$40. In most cases, jobs require a degree, a minimum of one to three years experience and excellent Excel skills.

Accountemps
601 Union St., #4300
Seattle WA 98101
(206) 749-9161
Fax: (206) 749-9243
http://www.accountemps.com
seattle@accountemps.com
Part of Robert Half International. Offers temporary placements in accounting and finance. In late 1997, was filling such positions as interim controller, accounting manager and Securities and Exchange Commission (SEC) specialist.

Accountemps
10900 N.E. 4th, #1650
Bellevue WA 98004
(425) 451-1000
Fax: (425) 455-1898
http://www.accoutemps.com
bellevue@accountemps.com

Accountemps
2505 S. 320th St., #120
Federal Way WA 98003
(253) 946-1776
Fax: (253) 946-2095
federalway@accountemps.com

Accountemps
3400 188th St. S.W., #165
Lynnwood WA 98037
(425) 712-7166
Does not accept unsolicited resumes by fax.

Accounting Partners
500 108th Ave. N.E., #1640
Bellevue WA 98004
(425) 450-1990
Fax: (425) 450-1056
http:/www.apartner.com
Specializes in accounting and finance, doing both temporary and permanent placements. Positions range from accounting clerk to controller, from data entry to financial analyst. Most upper level accounting positions are for staff accountants; you should have an accounting degree and one to three years experience. A CPA is an excellent credential, but not as important as the appropriate experience. Such positions pay $11-$15 an hour. A financial analyst should have at least two years experience; a degree is preferred. You'll also need proficiency with a spreadsheet management program. Almost all jobs require DOS or Windows. A junior analyst might make $10-$12 an hour, a more senior person $15-$25.

Accounting Quest
101 Stewart St., #1000
Seattle WA 98101
(206) 441-5600
Fax: (206) 441-5656
gregg@accountingquest.com
Contact: Greg Gillard, office director
Specialty: temporary and permanent positions in accounting and finance for high-technology and high-growth companies between Tacoma and Everett. Also offices in Portland and Denver. Positions range from accounting clerk to accounting manager, which might pay $40,000-$50,000, and controller, which might pay $50,000-$80,000; to senior financial analysts and finance directors, which might pay $40,000-$90,000; and to MIS systems implementation jobs, which might pay $35,000-$90,000. Lower-level positions require accounting education or fast data entry and a stable work history; for all positions, you'll need good references, evidence of progressively more responsible professional growth, a can-do attitude and enthusiasm. To apply, call or submit a resume (two pages maximum). Works on a contingency basis with all fees employer paid.

Allied Personnel Services
14900 Interurban Ave. S., #271
Seattle WA 98168
(206) 674-4563
Fax: (206) 674-4568
rnebeker@seanet.com
Contact: Robert Nebeker, president
A local firm established in 1995. Offers entry-level to experienced professionals on a contract and permanent basis in engineering (electrical, mechanical, structural and civil) and related technical fields (drafters, programmers and analysts, but no technical writers or graphic designers). All fees employer paid. How to apply: call first and then send your resume.

Alternative Resource Corp.
2001 Sixth Ave., #2100
Seattle WA 98121
(206) 441-9772
Fax: (206) 441-3431
http://www.alrc.com
Contact: Diana Smith, branch manager
Headquartered in Illinois. Provides technical resources to information technology companies in such areas as connectivity support, desktop computing, help desk, Internet/intranet, mainframe/midrange and voice and data communications.

Analysts International Corp.
10655 N.E. 4th St., #800
Bellevue WA 98004
(425) 454-2500
Fax: (425) 454-4288
http:/www.analysts.com/Seattle
seattle.jobs@analysts.com

Offers software consulting services with its in-house staff as well as contractors. Because many projects involve management consulting, the ideal candidate would have excellent communications and business management skills in addition to the technical expertise. Minimum: five years experience and a bachelor's degree. For some positions, a graduate degree (probably an MBA) is helpful. Headquartered in Minneapolis; serving Seattle since the mid-1980s. To apply, e-mail a resume.

Anchor Staffing

160 N.W. Gilman Blvd., #3
Issaquah WA 98027
(425) 837-1355
Fax: (425) 837-1715
anchor_sr@msn.com
Contact: Pamela Gotham, principal
Established in 1995, this local firm provides executive search for interim and permanent positions in sales, technology, manufacturing and accounting. Positions range from contract programmers in information systems to mid and senior management. Candidates for executive positions should have at least two years experience in that function. The agency also offers temporary and permanent placement in medical and health professions, entry-level to experienced. Typical positions: RNs, CNAs, physical therapists, speech pathologists and nurse practitioners. A third division offers placements in clerical and light industrial positions. All fees are employer paid. To apply, you can call, write or e-mail; your resume (scanner-legible, maximum two pages) will be filed for a year.

ArtSource Inc.

188 106th Ave. N.E., #400
Bellevue WA 98004
(425) 688-0094
Fax: (425) 688-0095
http://www.artsource.com
info@artsource.com
Contacts: Jeff and Melody Christensen
Established in 1993, this local firm provides online artists on a contract (usually three months) basis to Seattle and Eastside companies. Formal training (art school or a fine arts degree) is preferred and candidates must have Photoshop expertise. Skill with other illustration, web-authoring, desktop publishing and 3D programs is valuable, too. Entry-level employees can make $12-$15 an hour; experienced professionals might be paid as much as $50-$75. All fees are employer paid. To apply, submit a resume; if your skills fit the agency's current openings, you'll be interviewed.

BEST Consulting

12910 Totem Lake Blvd., #270
Kirkland WA 98034
(425) 814-8104
Fax: (425) 814-8108
http://www.bestnet.com
best@bestnet.com
Two divisions: Best Consulting has full-time employees who provide temporary

technical help for client companies in positions ranging from help-desk to C++ programmers. New Tech handles clients' computer problems on a turnkey basis, working from strategic planning to implementation.

Big Fish Promotions
605 Market St.
Kirkland WA 98033
(425) 827-8487, (800) 624-2863
Fax: (425) 827-8493
http://www.bigfishpromo.com
jeni@bigfishpromo.com
Contact: Jeni Herberger, co-owner
A local company founded in 1994, Big Fish provides creative communications professionals for online, interactive and print production on a free-lance, contract or permanent basis. Temporary placements range from four hours to more than two months. Typical positions: designers, photographers, animators and writers. Pay range: $28-$75 per hour. Candidates with formal education in their field and more than two years of professional experience are preferred, but interns can occasionally be placed. Fees are employer paid; applicants can contract with Big Fish for portfolio services, for which the job-seeker pays.

Bostwick Temporary Services
1109 First Ave., #406
Seattle WA 98101
(206) 340-1516
Fax: (206) 340-1522
bostwickinc@msn
Contact: (Mr.) Chris Bostwick, president
Legal positions, including contract attorneys (who, with experience and Washington state bar credentials, can make $30-$75 an hour), and administrative support positions are filled by this local agency. Positions may temporary or temp-to-hire. To apply, call for an appointment.

Butler International (Butler Service Group)
P.O. Box 4084
Bellevue WA 98009
(425) 885-6222
Fax: (425) 885-4988
http://www.butlerintl.com
cherbig@butlerintl.com
Contact: (Mr.) Chris Herbig
A national firm, Butler established a branch here in the late 1970s to provide contract engineering services, especially in aerospace. Contracts are often one to three years in length, with employees receiving some benefits from Butler. Candidates often need degrees in electrical, mechanical, aeronautical or stress engineering, with at least two years of experience. Typical pay rate: $30 per hour. All fees employer paid. To apply, mail in a scannable resume.

Career Clinic

9725 3rd Ave. N.E., #509
Seattle WA 98115
(206) 524-9831
Fax: (206) 524-4125
career@career.cnet.com

Established in 1967, this local agency fills temporary and permanent positions from support to senior level in four fields: high technology (for example, channel sales, network administrator, programmer), insurance (for example, claims manager or underwriter), construction (for example, estimator or project manager) and administrative support. Nearly all positions require at least three to five years of experience. Most fees are employer paid; check when you register. No unsolicited applications or resumes are accepted; call for an appointment.

Careers Northwest

3405 188th St. S.W., #102
Lynnwood WA 98037
(425) 778-3100; from Everett: (425) 347-2941; from Marysville: (360) 653-5367
Fax: (425) 774-5795
Contacts:
Administrative support: Brenda Williams, agency manager
Marketing and high technology: Ed Beaulieu, department manager
An affiliate of Business Careers.

CCZ Technical Service

3920 150th Ave. N.E.
Redmond WA 98052
(425) 881-6220
Fax: (425) 869-6311
http://www.ccz.com
ccz@ccz.com

Information technology and software engineering are the focus at this local firm, which provides both contract and permanent staff. Contractors can make from $15 an hour at entry-level to $50-$70 an hour; you'll need experience with the latest technology and, for testing applicants, experience with Windows testing. Employer paid fees. To apply, you can call or e-mail a resume.

CDI Corp. West

4030 Lake Washington Blvd. N.E., #210
Kirkland WA 98033
(425) 739-7800
Fax: (425) 739-7818
cdiwest@aol.com

Software engineers, drafters and technical writers are some of the positions filled on a contract basis. A degree isn't required for all positions, but a minimum of two or three years experience is. Seldom has entry-level openings. Employer paid fees. Resumes can be faxed or e-mailed in.

CDI Corp. West
4030 Lake Washington Blvd. N.E., #210
Kirkland WA 98033
(425) 739-7800
Fax: (425) 739-7818
cditek@aol.com
Hires technicians, assemblers, testers, quality control staff, machine operators and shipping and receiving crews on a contract or temp-to-hire basis. Employer paid fees.

CDI Corp. West
4040 Lake Washington Blvd. N.E., #101
Kirkland WA 98033
(425) 739-2100
Fax: (425) 739-7878
nparikh@cdicorp.com
Fills positions in information technology (for example, system integration and development, system analysis, LAN/WAN design, LAN support and project management) on a contract and contract-to-hire basis. A typical assignment is six months long. Usually requires a degree and at least two years experience. Occasional entry-level positions for new computer science graduates. Employer paid fees.

Church, Janet
See Janet Church & Associates

Cintech Corp.
335 Parkplace, #109
Kirkland WA 98033
(425) 828-6220
Fax: (425) 828-9697
http://www.cintech.com
resumes@cintech.com
Contact: Gary Cleveland, president
Focus: information technology, on a permanent or contract (three months or longer) basis. Typical positions: software engineer, UNIX systems administrator and technical writer. Most positions require a minimum of three years experience and at least a bachelor's degree; you'll be easier to place if you have at least five years experience. A recent software engineering graduate can expect to make about $36,000; an experienced technical writer can make $28-$30 an hour. To apply, submit a scannable resume; you can also respond to ads by telephone. A locally-owned firm established in 1993. All fees employer paid.

Coape Staffing Network
11400 S.E. 8th St., #205
Bellevue WA 98004
(425) 453-5576
Fax: (425) 453-6140
http://www.coapestaffing.com
donnah@coapestaffing.com
Contact: Donna Haslebacher, area manager

Affiliated with APPLEONE and owned by a San Diego company, this agency was established here in 1997 to offer contract and permanent placements in information technology. For engineering positions, you'll be easier to place if you have three to five years experience. Software testing usually requires a year or two of experience, although there are occasional entry-level opportunities. Work with computer hardware requires a B.S.E.E. or a B.S.M.E. Marketing management positions often require a technical bachelor's degree, an MBA and three to five years experience in product management. Permanent placements are done on a contingency basis; for contract placements (usually a minimum of six months), fees are employer paid. Makes placements in Seattle and on the Eastside from Kent to Everett. To apply, you can fax or e-mail a resume or call for information.

Comforce/RHOTECH
4002 148th Ave. N.E.
Redmond WA 98073
(425) 883-2233
Fax: (425) 869-9898
http://www.comforce.com
jobs@redmond.rhotech.com
Formerly the locally-owned RHO Co., this firm was merged into a national agency in 1997. Places people in positions ranging from entry-level clerical and light industrial to professional and technical. Most opportunities are in the software industry, in jobs such as tester or developer. Most upper-level positions require at least two to four years experience. Assignment length: one week to ongoing. To be added to Comforce's database, submit a cover letter identifying the positions you seek and a scannable resume. All fees employer paid.

CompuSearch
2510 Fairview Ave. E.
Seattle WA 98102
(206) 328-0936
Fax: (206) 328-3256
http://www.mrinet.com
seattle!jrg@mrinet.com
Contact: Dan Jilka, manager
Affiliated with Management Recruiters International, Seattle. Handles contract and permanent placements in software engineering and data processing. A typical position requires five to seven years experience, with a degree in computer science, electrical engineering or mechanical engineering preferred. Seventy per cent of the placements are local. All fees employer paid.

Computemp
11400 S.E. 8th, #235
Bellevue WA 98004
(425) 450-8899
Fax: (425) 450-9822
Contact: Jennifer Gebert, technical recruiter
Focus: information technology, including networking, software development and technical support. Offers temporary, contract and permanent placements. Most positions require at least a year of professional work experience; a technical degree

is helpful. An internship program for recent graduates and students. This is a franchise. All fees are employer paid. To apply, fax or e-mail a resume; if your background fits Computemp's needs, you'll be prescreened by telephone and possibly invited in for an interview.

Computer Group Inc.

P.O. Box 3424
Bellevue WA 98009-3424
(425) 455-3100
Fax: (425) 455-8445
http://www.computergroup.com
resumes@computergroup.com
Owned by the Utah-based SOS Staffing, this agency offers contract (six months or longer) and permanent placement in such high-tech positions as software developer and engineer, programmer analyst and web-site developers. Most positions require at least three years of experience, with five or 10 years experience and a computer science degree preferred. Makes placements between Portland and Everett, with an occasional job in eastern Washington. To apply, submit a scannable resume in reverse chronological format that describes your responsibilities on each job. All fees employer paid.

Computer People

1601 Fifth Ave., #800
Seattle WA 98101
(206) 628-0950
Fax: (206): 628-0258
http://www.computerpeople.com
recruiting.sea@cpeople.com
Based in Massachusetts. An international information systems firm with branches across the U.S., including here and in Portland. Places people on contract (usually at least three months). The ideal candidate will have three to five years experience; some clients require degrees. No entry-level positions. To apply, call the office or e-mail a resume.

Conmarke U.S.A. Inc.

18717 76th Ave. W., #I
Lynnwood WA 98037
(425) 712-1948
Fax: (425) 712-7087
This local marine construction and design firm leases employees (that means you're actually a Conmarke employee) in such fields as marine engineering, design and drafting. To apply, you'll need experience and Autocad expertise. Pay: usually $20-$30 an hour.

The Cordada Group

2310 130th Ave. N.E., #B-201
Bellevue WA 98005
(425) 869-4040
Fax: (425) 869-4070
http://www.cordada.com
Headquartered in Bellevue, also has a branch outside Portland. Established in

1991. Most work involves Internet applications, groupware solutions and client-server development. Places on a contract (90 per cent of the business) and permanent basis. Most contract assignments will extend to a year or longer. The ideal candidate will have three to five years experience and excellent customer service skills. To e-mail a resume, see the web site for instructions; mailed resumes must be scannable.

Creative Assets
101 Yesler Way, #200
Seattle WA 98104
(206) 682-6005
Fax: (206) 682-5830
http://www.creativeassets.com
resumesea@creativeassets.com
Handles computer graphic design and production, multimedia, desktop publishing and illustration. The ideal candidate has three to five years paid professional experience and a traditional graphic design background. Software expertise most in demand at press time: Photoshop. Most clients use Macs, although there are some Windows jobs. Jobs typically run about two months. A local firm with branches in Portland and San Francisco.

CTS Technical Services
11100 N.E. 8th, #510
Bellevue WA 98004
(425) 451-0051
Fax: 451-0052
http://www.ctstech.com
info@ctstech.com
Established in the mid-1980s, this local firm makes contract placements in aerospace (for example, engineers and drafters) and the computer industry (for example, developers, testers and localizers). You can submit a resume via fax or e-mail; if your background fits CTS's current needs, you'll be prescreened by telephone. See current openings on the web site. All fees employer paid.

Data Partners
11100 N.E. 8th, #350
Bellevue WA 98004
(425) 451-1030
Fax: (425) 451-9181
http://www.datapartners.com
wajobs@datapartners.com
Contact: Candace Gordon, branch manager
Focus: information technology, both contract (three months or longer) and permanent. Most jobs require a minimum of one to three years experience and a stable work history; for permanent positions, you'll probably need a computer science or business administration degree. To apply, call or submit a scannable resume. If you e-mail your resume, use a Word or WordPerfect document. A local firm, established in 1994.

Deloitte & Touche Re:sources Connection LLC
700 Fifth Ave., #4500
Seattle WA 98104
(206) 233-7635
Fax: (206) 343-7809
Http://www.dttus.com
jwonglee@dttus.com
Contact: Janie Lee, operations director
Established in 1996, this subsidiary of a major accounting firm has 10 offices on
the West Coast (including one in Portland) to provide interim professionals and
managers in accounting, finance and tax. This office makes placements across
Washington and in some other locations across the U.S. Most senior-level assignments (a CFO, for example) are two to six months in length and require several
years of public accounting and/or industry experience as well as a CPA or MBA.
Some such positions become permanent, with salaries in the $60,000-$100,000
range. A controller who has Big 6 and industry experience with a CPA might make
the equivalent of $45,000-$60,000. For professional-level positions in audit or tax,
projects often run from two weeks to six months; pay may start at $20 per hour. For
recent graduates with limited experience, there's occasionally an opportunity to
move from Re:sources to a regular Deloitte & Touche position. Some part-time
opportunities. All fees employer paid.

Eber Finance Inc.
600 University St., #2400
Seattle WA 98101
(206) 343-5390
Fax: (206) 624-7579
deber@wolfenet.com
Contact: Deena Eber
A CPA herself, Deena Eber specializes in executive search for accounting and
finance positions for such industries as telecommunications, software, and
biotechnology. Positions range from staff accountant and accounting manager to
CFO. In finance, where positions often need an MBA, opportunities might range
from analyst to director or vice president. Occasional contract opportunities; a job-
share can sometimes be structured when a candidate wishes to work part-time. To
have your resume added to Eber's database, submit it by mail, e-mail or fax; do not
telephone. Eber works on a contingency basis.

Engineering Corp. of America
2705 California Ave. S.W.
Seattle WA 98116
(206) 932-0654
Fax: (206) 932-1754
http://www.ecofa.com
eca@ecofa.com
Contacts:
Greg Zanghi, computer science
Marcia Sheckler, engineering
Specialty: contract and contract-to-hire positions in software, civil and mechanical
engineering, mostly in the Seattle area. Locally-owned, with branches in Everett
(see below) and Portland. All fees employer paid.

Engineering Corp. of America
P.O. Box 5546
Everett WA 98206
(425) 252-9635
Fax: (425) 258-3285
http://www.ecofa.com
al@ecanorth.com

FDSI Consulting/Cotelligent
P.O. Box 3008
Bellevue WA 98009-3008
(425) 637-6505
Fax: (425) 637-1805
http://www.cotl.com
jobs-wa@cotl.com
Contact: Jill Hansell, vice president, Recruiting Services
Specialty: contract and permanent positions in such information technology positions as project manager, software engineer and business process analyst. Many positions require three to five years minimum experience in a programming language; a degree is helpful. Candidates also should understand such client needs as database marketing. Headquartered in Bellevue, this firm also has a Portland office.

Franklin Search Group
See Medzilla/The Franklin Search Group

Hall Kinion
3001 112th Ave. N.E., #101
Bellevue WA 98004
(425) 889-5003
Fax: (425) 889-5985
http://www.hallkinion.com
hallkinb@ix.netcom.com
Contact: Debbie Allen Oberbillig, manager, Technical Recruiting
A branch of a San Jose firm, this organization focuses on such contract and permanent high technology positions as research and development software engineers, testers and network administrators. Most positions require a bachelor's degree and one to five years experience. On a permanent basis, a software engineer with five years experience might make $60,000; a more experienced person at a senior level might earn $80,000.

Hallmark Placements
1904 Third Ave., #819
Seattle WA 98101
(206) 587-5360
Fax: (206) 587-5319
Contact: Dolores Gohndrone, manager
Focus: temporary and permanent placements in engineering for the software industry (often requiring a degree in electrical engineering or computer science), food service (including bartenders, chefs and management) and administration

(from clerks to accounting managers). Most positions pay $60,000 or less. Most engineering jobs require five to 10 years experience, most sales jobs three to five years similar experience and the most senior level accounting positions require at least five years experience. At the lower level, half of the fees are paid by the job-seeker; check when you apply. To apply, call for an appointment. Lower level positions require skills testing. Locally owned; founded in 1981.

HR Services Inc.
1001 Fourth Ave., #3200
Seattle WA 98154
(206) 340-1471
Fax: (206) 340-0113
http://www.aa.net/hrservices
hrsvcs@aa.net
Contact: Victoria Cobos, president
Human resources positions (from recruiters, compensation specialist and benefits analysts to managers) on a temporary (three months or longer) and permanent basis are the specialty of this local firm established in 1988. Some part-time opportunities, both temporary and permanent. Most positions require four to seven years corporate (rather than employment agency) experience, a degree and CEBS or equivalent certification. Temporary assignments pay $14-$30 an hour, permanent positions $35,000-$75,000. All fees employer paid.

Human Resource Alternatives
4040 Lake Washington Blvd., #105
Kirkland WA 98033
(425) 739-4300
Fax: (425) 739-7848
A division of CDI. Provides human resources professionals (HR specialist to director) on a contract (two or three months minimum) and permanent basis. Some positions become temp-to-hire. Typical pay is $25 an hour; a senior recruiter might make $40 an hour. A HR assistant position will require a year of similar experience; most positions require a degree and at least three years experience in human resources. Candidates include those who are between jobs, those currently employed but seeking a change and HR consultants who want an agency to market them. To apply, submit a cover letter and resume; you'll be interviewed if your skills match client needs. You may be interviewed faster if you've been referred by a client. All fees employer paid.

Information Technology Services Inc.
2310 130th Ave. N.E., #B-201
Bellevue WA 98005
(425) 869-4040
http://www.itservices.com
Provides software consulting on a contract basis. Candidates should have at least four years high-tech experience.

Intelligent Life
3513 N.E. 45th St., Mezzanine Level
Seattle WA 98105
(206) 812-0786
Fax: (206) 812-0793
http://www.int-life.com
info@int-life.com
Contact: Beryl Gorbman
Locally owned, this firm focuses on new media: for example, web site developers, audio/video editors, digital media, audio mixers, video and film production and computer graphics. At a minimum, candidates should have a year or two of relevant experience. Degrees are helpful. To apply, watch for newspaper or web site ads for the type of job you seek.

Janet Church & Associates
101 Stewart St., #300
Seattle WA 98101
(206) 443-9673
Fax: (206) 443-9674
http://www.jcai.com
Contact: (Ms.) J. Jones
High-tech marketing and event management firm which hires consultants on a contract basis. Some work for a few days, others for much longer in positions ranging from project manager to marketing director. Most positions require at least five years experience in software industry management; a thorough understanding of software distribution is preferred.

Kelly Technical
700 Fifth Ave., #4125
Seattle WA 98104
(206) 382-1656
Fax: (206) 382-9679
http://www.kellyservices.com
kellysea@ix.netcom.com
One of Kelly Services' 10 Puget Sound offices. Focus: high tech industry positions, including information technology, technical (aeronautical, electrical, industrial and mechanical engineers, CAD and traditional drafters, product planners and schedulers), and related professionals (including buyers, technical writers and computer hardware and software curriculum designers). Positions may be temp-to-hire, contract (although seldom less than a month in length) or permanent. Clients range from Bellingham to Centralia. What does a candidate need? A degree is preferred and so is recent related work experience (one year minimum, with at least three years preferred). You'll also need at least two references and a stable work history (recruiters prefer to see two or three years in each job). To apply, you can e-mail or mail a scannable resume (see Kelly's web site for a template). All fees employer paid.

Law Dawgs

1201 Third Ave., #2810
Seattle WA 98101
(206) 224-8244
Fax: (206) 224-8291
http://www.jetcity.com/~lawdawgs.html
lawdawgs@jetcity.com
Contact: Ewen Cameron, president
Places legal professionals, including paralegals and contract attorneys, on a temporary, temp-to-hire and permanent basis in law firms and corporations. Some attorneys work as long as eight months on contract; some are hired after working on contract. A local firm established in 1995. To apply, call for more information; applicants are screened prior to being interviewed. All fees employer paid.

Legal Ease LLC

615 Market St., #B
Kirkland WA 98033
(425) 822-1157
Fax: (425) 889-2775
http://www.legalease.com
legalease@legalease.com
Contact: Lynda Jonas, Esq., principal
Matches attorneys who work on an independent contractor basis with law firms, corporations and government legal departments. Most work is contract—for an afternoon or an ongoing part-time assignment. Some permanent placements. Occasionally places paralegals, often law school graduates or attorneys who are willing to handle paralegal-level assignments. A local firm established in 1996 that serves the greater Puget Sound area. Any law school graduate or paralegal can be interviewed; call or e-mail Lynda Jonas for an appointment. Candidates are easier to place when they have two or three years of experience and if they graduated in the upper half of their class. For permanent placement, some clients look at the law school attended. All fees employer paid.

Linda Werner & Associates

318 W. Galer St.
Seattle WA 98119
(206) 281-9069
Fax: (206) 281-9068
http://www.lwerner.com
placements@lwerner.com
Places publication professionals in high-tech companies on a contract (usually three months or longer) and permanent basis. Positions include technical writers and editors, programmer writers, web programmers, instructional designers, technical illustrators, desktop publishers and graphic designers. Candidates should have three to five years experience; degrees are preferred, especially for permanent placements. To submit your credentials, e-mail in a resume as an attachment. All fees employer paid.

Macrosearch

13353 Bel-Red Rd., #206
Bellevue WA 98005
(425) 641-7252
Fax: (425) 641-0969
http://www.macrosearch.com
macro@macrosearch.com
Contact: Margie Peterson, president
Founded in 1989, this local firm places information technology professionals and managers on a contract and permanent basis across most of the state. Occasional entry-level opportunities (for software testing, for example) that can be filled by college students. Some temporary jobs (technical writer, web developer, network administrator, PC support) can be handled after usual office hours. For project managers, a technical background is valuable, even if the job isn't hands-on; industry and consulting experience are also helpful. Pay for these jobs: $40,000-$100,000. Most placements are for very experienced high-level technical professionals (a programmer or software engineer, for example). To apply, call and then submit a scanner-readable resume (reverse chronological format preferred). All fees employer paid.

MacTemps

520 Pike St., #1340
Seattle WA 98101
(206) 622-2800
Fax: (206) 622-6426
http://www.mactemps.com
Contact: Tom Linde, market manager
Focus: computer graphics and electronic pre-press. Candidates often need expertise in Quark XPress, Photoshop, PageMaker, Illustrator and Freehand. Affiliated with Portfolio and 1-800-NETWORK. Contract and temporary placements. All fees employer paid.

Manpower Technical Division

911 5th Ave., #102
Kirkland WA 98033
(425) 889-9745
Fax: (425) 822-8708
http://www.manpower.com
Contact: Carla Scharb, manager
Headquartered in Milwaukee, Manpower has owned offices in the Puget Sound area for decades. Between Olympia and Bellingham, there are 11 plus client-satellites. You should register with the office that serves your geographic area unless you're applying for technical jobs, which are all placed from Kirkland regardless of where you register. This office recruits across the U.S. for Puget Sound-area clients. The most common openings are for programmers (SQL, UNIX, C++) who might earn $20-$60 an hour, network specialists who might earn a minimum of $18-$25, and help desk support staff, who make $15-$25. The office also handles positions ranging from desktop publishing (70 per cent PC-based), technical writers and editors, CAD specialists, software engineers and systems analysts. Temporary, temp-to-hire and permanent. All fees employer paid.

Maritime Employment Services Inc.

74 S. Lucille
Seattle WA 98134
(206) 767-5180
Fax: (206) 767-5288
http://www.maritimemployment.com
jobs@maritimemployment.com
Founded in 1988, this local firm places crews (factory to licensed wheelhouse staff) on fishing, deep sea, cruise, casino and towing vessels. Temporary (perhaps just a few weeks) and permanent. Fees are paid by job applicants. To apply, call for an appointment.

Maritime Recruiters

P.O. Box 260
Mercer Island WA 98040
(206) 232-6041
Fax: (206) 232-6041
Contact: Bob Walton, senior partner
Since 1969, making permanent (90 per cent of the business) and contract placements in the maritime industry. Only about 10 per cent of the jobs are seagoing; others may be in naval architecture, admiralty law, engineering, design of marine machinery, operations, offshore oil drilling, shipyard management and trades, finance, marine insurance and translation (Russian, Japanese and Chinese). Most positions require at least five years experience. To apply, submit a resume (reverse chronological format). If your background matches the firm's current needs, you'll be screened by telephone. All fees employer paid.

Micropath Inc.

2353 130th Ave. N.E., #110
Bellevue WA 98005
(425) 702-1887
Fax: (425) 702-3730
http://www.micropathinc.com
hr@micropathinc.com
Headquartered in Bellevue, with branches elsewhere in the U.S. Uses permanent and contract staff to provide "computer asset management," inventorying hardware and software for clients and making recommendations regarding integration and migration. Many positions require experience, but recent college graduates can be used on some contracts. To apply, fax or e-mail a resume.

Millennium Staffing

601 Union St., #1625
Seattle WA 98101
(206) 464-4055
Fax: (206) 464-4147
millennium@seanet.com
Contact: Steve Curran, staffing consultant
Part of a national launched in 1997; affiliated with Accountants On Call. Provides project and permanent placement of "administrative and creative services professionals" for web-site and desktop publishing creation and higher-level administra-

tive support. Candidates need to be able to communicate well and have strong software and creative skills. How to approach: send in your resume first; the most qualified candidates will be interviewed.

Mindpower Inc.

8440 154th Ave. N.E.
Redmond WA 98052
(425) 556-9600
Fax: (425) 556-1771
http://www.mindpower-inc.com
hr@mindpower-inc.com
Contact: (Mr.) Nilesh Shah, president
Specialty: contract (typically three months) and permanent placement of technical staff, ranging from entry-level technicians and help desk support to engineers and software and hardware designers. Help desk jobs may pay $10-$12; senior level programmers can make $50-$70. For contract jobs, experience is more important than education; for permanent positions, employers often want a B.S. in computer science. Locally owned; founded in 1997.

Mini-Systems Associates

14535 Bel-Red Rd., #200
Bellevue WA 98007
(425) 644-9500
Fax: (425) 644-0200
http://www.mini-systems.com/msa
resumes@wa.mini-systems.com
A branch of a California firm. Provides contract (two weeks to several months) and permanent placements in high technology, including software developers, engineers and testers, technical writers and telecommunications splicers, technicians and installers. For software positions, there's little entry-level work. Pay may be $20-40 an hour.

Minzel & Associates

1191 Second Ave., #1900
Seattle WA 98101
(206) 689-8526
Fax: (206) 628-9506
m-and-a@msn.com
Contact: Jeff Minzel
Provides attorneys and paralegals on a temporary and temp-to-hire basis to government agencies, law firms and corporations. To apply, fax your resume; if your background meets the firm's current needs, you'll be interviewed.

Morgen Design Inc.

150 Andover Park W.
Seattle WA 98188
(206) 433-7863
Fax: (206) 433-8809
http://www.w-link.net/~morgen
morgen@w-link.net
Contacts:
Elaine Tsang, employment specialist, engineering
Sylvia Washington, employment specialist, laborers
Headquartered in Salt Lake City, this firm has two divisions: an in-house engineering office, for which it hires permanent and contract employees, and the placement agency. Engineering jobs require experience and a degree in electrical, aeronautical or mechanical engineering. Also places some laborers and clerical staff. Employer paid fees.

Nelson, Coulson & Associates

14450 N.E. 29th Pl., #115
Bellevue WA 98007
(425) 883-6612
Fax: (425) 883-6916
http://www.ncainc.com
denise@ncainc.com
Contact: Denise Buettgenbach, manager
A branch of a Denver firm. Focus: high technology, including aerospace engineers, electronic technicians, administrative assistants and customer service staff. Places on a temporary (two or three months or longer), contract (six months to several years) and permanent basis. Typical pay: an aerospace engineer with five to 10 years experience and a degree might make $35 an hour on contract. Works on a contingency basis.

Opus Corp.

P.O. Box 50088
Bellevue WA 98015
(425) 688-1904
Fax: (425) 688-1957
resumes@opusco.com
Contact: Robina Werner, president
Founded in late 1997. Locally owned. Provides high tech staff in Washington and northern Oregon. About 50 per cent of placements are contract (three months or longer); the balance are permanent. The ideal candidate: at least three to five years experience. A degree is preferred. All fees employer paid. To apply, e-mail a resume that shows attention to detail and a description of your accomplishments.

Parfitt Recruiting & Consulting

P.O. Box 1932
Bellevue WA 98009
(425) 636-6300
Fax: (425) 643-6411
http://www.prcsearch.com
prc@prcsearch.com
Contact: Jan Parfitt, vice president
This local search firm, established in 1987, specializes in information technology
and information systems, filling senior positions that pay from $40,000. Both
contract and permanent placements. Works both on contingency and retainer basis.

Personnel Consultants

14042 N.E. 8th, #201-B
Bellevue WA 98007
(425) 641-0657
Fax: (425) 641-0657
buzy73A@prodigy.com
Contact: Larry Dykes, recruiter
Specialty: the insurance industry, including positions in claims, risk management,
actuarial, underwriting and sales and marketing for brokers and carriers. Both
temporary (often several months) and permanent placements. Most positions
require six or more years industry experience. All fees employer paid.

Portfolio

520 Pike St., #1350
Seattle WA 98101
(206) 623-3800
Fax: (206) 623-3866
http://www.portfolio.skill.com
Contact: Tom Linde, market manager
A division of MacTemps. Also affiliated with 1-800-NETWORK. Places interface
designers, multimedia programmers, content developers (writers) and 3-D animators. Contract work.

Programming & Consulting Services, Inc.

16040 Christensen Rd., #110
Tukwila WA 98188
(206) 241-5113, (800) 995-8917
Fax: (206) 241-5192
http://www.pcs-northwest.com
psc@siteconnect.com
Specialty: information services, both contract (two weeks to two years) and
permanent. Positions range from help desk and PC installers to project managers.
Most positions require at least three years experience. Seldom any entry-level jobs.
A local firm, established in 1977. Also has Portland and Olympia offices:

Programming & Consulting Services, Inc.
509 E. 12th Ave., #4
Olympia WA 98501
(360) 352-1517, (800) 226-0567
Fax: (360) 352-0425
http://www.pcs-northwest.com
marypcs@aol.com

Pyramid Technical Services
3006 Northup Way, #301
Bellevue WA 98004
(425) 822-1182
Fax: (425) 822-0412
http://www.pyramidtech.com
jobs@pyramidtech.com
Contact: Jerry Reed, president
Accepts applications from high tech professionals (software engineers, technical
writers, computer operators and data communications staff) seeking contract and
permanent positions. A resume can be e-mailed as an attachment to a cover letter.
Established in 1992. All fees employer paid.

Q Corp.
320 108th Ave. N.E., #600
Bellevue WA 98004
(425) 635-7812
Fax: (425) 454-8902
aradhnaf@msn.com
This high-tech consulting firm specializes in client-server development, placing
professionals on a contract basis (three months to a year). Most candidates need to
have at least two years full-time professional experience in addition to their
academic projects. A local firm established in the early 1990s.

Resource Management Services
1501 Fourth Ave., #450
Seattle WA 98101
(206) 223-8991
Fax: (206) 223-8227
resourcemgt@msn.com
Contact: Suzanne Coleman, executive administrator
Affiliated with Parker Services. Places technical professionals and managers on an
interim and permanent basis in such service organizations as health care, retail,
financial services and hospitality (including web site designers, network administrators and content developers). Also places nontechnical managers in high tech
companies in such jobs as finance (including controllers and financial analysts),
human resources and marketing and communications (including advertising managers and sales representatives). Most positions require a degree and at least five
years experience. Candidates should have word processing, database management,
spreadsheet management and Internet expertise. Salary range: $35,000-$85,000.
All fees employer paid.

Re:sources Connection LLC
See Deloitte & Touche Re:sources Connection LLC

Resource Technology Group, Inc.
600 108th Ave. N.E., #237
Bellevue WA 98004
(425) 453-8500
Fax: (425) 688-7477
http://www.rtginc.com
The technical services arm of Northwest Temporary & Staffing Services, a Portland-based firm. Offers contract help with technical, engineering, data communications and telecommunications jobs, including Autocad and data processing. All fees employer paid.

RHI Consulting
601 Union St., #4300
Seattle WA 98101
(206) 749-0960
Fax: (206) 749-9373
http://www.rhic.com
seattle@rhic.com
Part of the Robert Half International organization. Focus: contract positions (often three to six months) in information technology, including testing engineers, PC/LAN technicians, technical writers and network administrators. Entry-level candidates can be placed if they have applicable skills. To apply, submit a resume; if your skills fit the firm's needs, you'll be interviewed and possibly tested. All fees employer paid.

RHI Consulting
10900 N.E. 4th St., #1650
Bellevue WA 98004
(425) 450-1951
Fax: (425) 455-1898
http://www.rhic.com
bellevue@rhic.com

RSA International
5200 Southcenter Blvd., #25
Seattle WA 98188
(206) 244-0554
Fax: (206) 243-3795
http://www.rsa-intl.com
rsa@rsa-intl.com
Contact: (Ms.) Sandy Antezana
Focus: information technology jobs in the Seattle area. Most (90 per cent) are permanent. The ideal candidate has a degree in computer science and two to three years programming language experience. Most openings pay $40,000 or more. Works on a contingency basis.

S & T Onsite
4300 Aurora Ave. N., #100
Seattle WA 98103
(206) 632-6931
Fax: (206) 632-6927
http://www.sakson.com/onsite
onsite@sakson.com
Contact: Dan Green
Specializes in contract work in technical communications, placing technical writers, copy editors, proofreaders, indexers, graphic designers and multimedia whizzes. Most work is in software documentation and online help. Candidates need experience in commercial (rather than in-house) software documentation and, in most jobs, Microsoft Word (Windows). Most opportunities are for technical writers, who need a technical background and writing experience, preferably in software or telecommunications documentation (pay range: $25-$45 an hour) and editors, who have both a technical background and editing experience (pay range: $18-$25 an hour). Resumes should be submitted via e-mail in Microsoft Word. All fees employer paid. Affiliated with Sakson & Taylor, a consulting firm specializing in documentation.

SDC Computer Services
4020 Lake Washington Blvd., #210
Kirkland WA 98033
(425) 889-0777
Fax: (425) 889-0300
http://www.supdes/seattle
sdc@sea.supdes.com
A subsidiary of Superior Design, headquartered in Buffalo, N. Y. In Washington since 1986. Handles contract assignments (averaging one year in length) in aerospace engineering, technical writing and software (for both programmers and technicians). To submit your credentials, e-mail a resume with cover letter.

Sea People
4005 20th Ave. W.
Seattle WA 98199
(206) 283-6595
Fax: (206) 283-6395
Contact: Michelle Gray
Specialty: temporary, contract and permanent positions in commercial fishing (80 per cent of the business) and such other maritime work as tugs and charters. Positions range from captains, mates and engineers to factory jobs, deckhands and land-based cooks. Occasional entry-level opportunities. Candidates can walk in or mail a resume. Most fees are paid by job-seekers.

The Select Group
2731 77th Ave. S.E.
Mercer Island WA 98040
(206) 236-2700
Fax: (206) 236-2704
http://www.select-group.com
bobcull@accessone.com
Contact: Bob Cullen, president
For information technology firms, handles contract (usually a three-month minimum) and permanent positions such as testers, programmers, technical writers and engineers.

Snelling Personnel Services
15 S. Grady Way, #246
Renton WA 98055
(425) 228-6500; from Bellevue: (425) 455-3117; from Seattle: (206) 621-7967
Fax: (425) 228-8661
snelling15@aol.com
Contact: Joan Dubie
A franchise, but not otherwise affiliated with other Snelling offices. Same owner since 1969. Focus: light industrial and administrative (general office to office manager) on a temporary or permanent basis. Also handles contract engineering jobs. Application procedure for engineering: fax a resume. All fees employer paid.

Source Services
500 108th N.E., #1780
Bellevue WA 98004
(425) 454-6400
Fax: (425) 688-0154
http://www.cnw.com/sourcedp
sourcedp@cnw.com
A branch of a national firm. Specialty: contract (three months and longer) and permanent placements in high technology. Many opportunities require a degree and at least two years experience. Openings across most of Washington state. To apply, call for information or submit a resume by fax or e-mail (use Word 6.0 or a text file). All fees employer paid. May add accounting and finance placements in early 1998.

TAD Resources International, Inc.
15 S. Grady Way, #509
Renton WA 98055
(425) 226-8333, (800) 532-0368
Fax: (425) 226-8374
http://www.tadseattle.com
jobs@tadseattle.com
This firm has three local offices, with all contract technical jobs—engineers, drafters, software professionals—being placed from this location. Applicants need at least two years applicable experience and, for engineers, CAD experience. Jobs often last one to three years. All fees employer paid. To apply, you can submit a resume and follow up with a phone call.

TCB Industrial Corp.
14900 Interurban S., #274
Seattle WA 98168
(206) 241-6296
Fax: (206) 241-6687
Contact: Brad Schroeder, vice president, Washington operations
Specialty: providing hazardous wastes specialists on a leased, temporary or temp-to-hire basis. Employees may work on hazardous materials accident clean-up or on Super Fund sites, as biologists, industrial hygienists, geologists, hydrologists, lab technicians, ship cleaning and repair or in administration of hazardous waste programs. Qualifications vary, but at a minimum all candidates must have completed the 40-hour OSHA Hazardous Wastes Operation and Emergency Response certification (HAZWOPER) program. To apply, call for an appointment or mail in a resume. All fees employer paid.

Technical Communications Plus
2110 N. 60th St.
Seattle WA 98103
(206) 729-0393
Fax: (206) 729-0393
http://www.tcplus.com
jatc@gte.net
Specialty: temporary assignments in technical communications (for example, for technical writers and editors and instructional designers). Does not place illustrators. You'll need at least two to five years applicable experience. All fees are employer paid.

Techstaff Inc.
720 Olive Way, #1510
Seattle WA 98101
(206) 382-5555
Fax: (206) 382-5556
http://www.crstech.com
Handles contract (two days to three years) and permanent placement in information technology, architecture and engineering. Seldom has demand for entry-level candidates; most positions require experience ranging from one to two years to 15 to 20 years of increasing responsibility. All fees employer paid. To apply, either call when you've seen an appropriate position advertised by the firm or mail in a resume.

Terra Technical Services
8625 Evergreen Way, #203
Everett WA 98208
(425) 355-7223; from Seattle: (206) 745-5141; toll-free: (800) 755-7638
Fax: (425) 353-1612
http://www.terrasvc.com
resume@terrasvc.com
Places engineers, drafters and computer professionals on a temporary basis. All fees employer paid.

Thompson and Associates Inc.

2448 76th Ave. S.E., #212
Mercer Island WA 98040
(206) 236-0153
Fax: (206) 236-2262
http://www.jobsnorthwest.com
neal@jobsnorthwest.com
Contact: Neal Thompson, president
Places technical people in high technology, manufacturing and service organizations in western Washington on a contract and permanent basis. Most positions require at least two years experience in the kind of job you seek. Established in 1981. Works on a contingency basis.

Volt Engineering and Technical Services

22232 17th Ave. S.E., #308
Bothell WA 98021
(425) 806-1900
Fax: (425) 806-1920
ecoleman@voltservgrp.com
Contact: Ed Coleman, branch manager
Headquartered in Orange, Calif., this employment agency has five divisions in the Seattle area. This division handles contract and permanent placement of machinists, inspectors, technical writers and editors, desktop publishers, planners and schedulers. To apply, submit your resume; applicants whose expertise meets Volt's needs will be screened by telephone or interviewed. All fees employer paid.

Volt Engineering and Technical Division

16400 Southcenter Parkway, #201
Seattle WA 98188
(206) 575-8455
Fax: (206) 575-3108
Contact: Lori Larson, area manager
Makes contract (usually six months or longer) and temp-to-hire placements of engineers (including stress and propulsion), computer professionals (including web site and software developers), and technical staff (including welders and fabricators). Few entry-level opportunities. Many positions require aerospace experience. To apply, submit your resume; applicants whose expertise meets Volt's needs will be screened by telephone or interviewed. All fees employer paid.

Volt Computer Services

8461 154th Ave. N.E.
Redmond WA 98052
(425) 702-9000
Fax: (425) 702-0315
www.volt-nw.com
resumes@volt-nw.com
Contact: Mark Prince, branch manager
Contract and permanent placement of such positions as programmer, analyst, network administrator, network support, web site developer, software tester and

configuration manager. Most positions require some experience. Electronic applications encouraged. All fees employer paid.

Volt Computer Services
9840 Willows Rd. N.E., #201
Redmond WA 98052
(425) 702-9600
Fax: (425) 558-9855
www.volt-tech.com

Volt Computer Services
16400 Southcenter Parkway, #201
Seattle WA 98188
(206) 575-8455
Fax: (206) 575-3108
www.volt-tech.com
dpalileo@voltsergp.com
Most positions filled by this office require a minimum of one or two years work experience. All fees employer paid.

Waldron Resources
101 Stewart St., #1200
Seattle WA 98101
(206) 727-9797
Fax: (206) 441-5213
Contact: Greg Prothman, vice president
Places interim professionals and managers in public sector positions.

Washington Contract Attorneys Group
14810 216th Ave. N.E.
Woodinville WA 98072
(206) 224-4459
Lawyers interested in working on a contract or temporary basis can join this group, which began as a spin-off of the state bar association's Lawyers' Assistance Program. Issues a quarterly directory (and monthly updates) of attorneys seeking contract work.

Washington Firm Ltd.
2 Nickerson, Courtyard Suite
Seattle WA 98109
(206) 284-4800
Fax: (206) 270-0410
http://www.wafirm.com
resumes1@wafirm.com
Contact: Al Battson, principal
This local firm has three divisions. One unit works on a retainer basis to place senior managers. A second group provides human resources staff on a project basis; both permanent and contract staff are hired for this. A third unit, Managed

Staffing, uses full-time employees and an occasional contract employee on teams in high tech firms to handle information systems, information technology, engineering, software and telecommunications projects. Established in 1981. All fees employer paid.

Wasser Inc.
2005 Fifth Ave., #201
Seattle WA 98121
(206) 441-0707
Fax: (206) 441-6628
http://www.wasserinc.com
Contact: Keith Martin, staffing recruiter
Specialty: out-sourcing and temporary staffing in technical communications, including writer/programmers, translator-localizers, technical editors, indexers, proofreaders, graphic designers, web-site developers and desktop publishers.

Werner, Linda
See Linda Werner & Associates

WesTech
1200 112th Ave. N.E., #C-110
Bellevue WA 98004
(425) 451-3848
Fax: (425) 637-9793
Places engineering, computer software and manufacturing production staff on a temporary, temp-to-hire and contract basis. Engineering positions include technical writers and illustrators, technicians, drafters, designers and electrical, mechanical, structural, civil, aerospace and chemical engineers. Pay varies from $28-$40 an hour for entry-level engineers to $60-$80 for senior professionals. Computer jobs range from help desk to programmers; candidates should have completed a certification program or a college degree or have significant experience. A recent computer science graduate might earn $35,000-$45,000. Most manufacturing production positions are for skilled workers and professionals rather than managers. An assembler can make $7.50-$12 an hour. Because some entry-level positions don't require much communication, they are appropriate for candidates with limited English skills. A technician, especially a graduate of a two-year technical program, can start at $9-$11 an hour and eventually make as much as $20. To apply, call for a telephone screening or fax in your resume with a letter indicating the kind of job you seek. Affiliated with Nu West. All fees employer paid.

Woods & Associates
1221 Second Ave., #430
Seattle WA 98101
(206) 623-2930
Fax: (206) 623-1216
A local firm established in 1987. Places administrative staff in legal, financial and health care support positions. Paralegals are usually the highest level positions filled. Placements may be temporary, contract or permanent. To apply, call for an appointment, which may take 90 minutes or more. All fees employer paid.

The Write Stuff
4534 1/2 University Way N.E.
Seattle WA 98105
(206) 548-1111
Fax: (206) 548-9116
http://www.writestuff.com
resume@writestuff.com
Specializes in technical writing and translating, web site design and production; uses technical writers and editors, localizers, indexers, instructional designers, illustrators, project managers, documentation assistants and production specialists. Places on a contract (can be two hours, but often three months) and occasionally on a permanent basis. Positions require a minimum of three years work experience. At press time the greatest demand was for programmer-writers, usually experienced programmers with technical writing skills. Pay ranges from $15 (for a proofreader) to $50 an hour. To apply, e-mail a resume and cover letter.

7. Industry Specialists

You're a writer, an architect, a franchise marketing wizard. You're an attorney or doctor, scientist, teacher or underwriter, ship captain or pharmaceutical sales rep. You speak Japanese or Chinese. Or perhaps you work in construction, government, nonprofits, hospitality or the automotive industry. This chapter, intended to highlight those local placement professionals who serve very specialized niches, lists those who work in markets and functions other than (or in addition to) high technology, accounting and finance. To be included here, a search firm must handle at least some senior professional or management positions on a permanent basis. All of the firms listed here are included (often with more detailed descriptions) in chapters such as *Executive Search Firms: Locally Based, Contract Employment* or *Employment Agencies*.

ACS & Associates
2835 82nd Ave. S.E., #201
Mercer Island WA 98040
(206) 728-8028
Fax: (206) 236-8104
ACSTEC@aol.com
Contact: Carl Smith, principal
A local executive search firm established in 1986. Usually paid on a retainer basis. Two specialties: the high tech industry, mostly for technical and financial positions; and the public sector, for management jobs and such staff positions as human resources. How to approach: send a resume (two pages maximum) with a cover letter that describes the position you seek, your salary expectations and whether you'll relocate.

Automotive Personnel
1800 136th Pl. N.E., #4
Bellevue WA98005
(425) 643-4788
Contact: Mark Johnson, owner
Established in the mid-1980s, this local firm specializes in the auto industry, recruiting staff for car dealerships. Positions range from lot attendants ($6-$7 an hour) to service cashiers, title clerks, technicians, finance and insurance specialists and salespeople. A general manager might be paid $100,000 or more, with the majority of the compensation in bonus form. Minimum qualifications: excellent driving record and clean police record. All fees are employer paid. Call for an appointment.

Barbara Ruhl & Associates
15 Diamond F Ranch
Bellevue WA 98004
(425) 453-7299
Fax: (425) 453-7801
Contact: Barbara Ruhl
This local search firm, founded in 1991, handles positions in mortgage, escrow and property management. All fees employer-paid. Unsolicited resumes are accepted if they don't exceed two pages and are scannable.

Big Fish Promotions
605 Market St.
Kirkland WA 98033
(425) 827-8487, (800) 624-2863
Fax: (425) 827-8493
http://www.bigfishpromo.com
jeni@bigfishpromo.com
Contact: Jeni Herberger, co-owner
A local company founded in 1994, Big Fish provides creative communications professionals for online, interactive and print production on a free-lance, contract or permanent basis. Typical positions: designers, photographers, animators and writers. Pay range: $28-$75 per hour. Candidates with formal education in their field and more than two years of professional experience are preferred, but interns can occasionally be placed. Fees are employer paid; applicants can contract with Big Fish for portfolio services, for which the job-seeker pays.

Black & Deering
1605 116th Ave. N.E., #211
Bellevue WA 98004
(425) 646-0905
Fax: (425) 451-0335
Contact: George Deering
Health care institutions—acute medical and surgical—are the focus of this local retained search firm, which places department managers to CEOs. Most positions do not require medical degrees, although many candidates have nursing as well as management experience. Serves Washington, Oregon, Idaho and Montana. Typical base salaries are $65,000-$115,000, with performance-based compensation packages increasingly common. If you submit a resume, it should be scannable and no more than two pages in length; it'll be retained for six months.

Catholic Archdiocese of Seattle
Office of the Superintendent of Schools
910 Marion St.
Seattle WA 98104
(206) 382-4856
Fax: (206) 654-4651
http://www.csdseattle.org
csd@connectinc.com
Distributes application packets for those interested in teaching in 64 Puget Sound Catholic schools. Maintains applicants' files and publicizes teaching openings with a weekly bulletin. Each year, handles 120-140 permanent openings, which are

filled after interviews at the individual schools. Also posts openings for substitute teachers.

Clevenger, Susan
See Susan Clevenger Executive Search

Construction Management Services
40 Lake Bellevue Dr., #100
Bellevue WA 98005
(425) 868-2211
Fax: (425) 868-6622
http://www.cms-seattle.com
Contact: Mark Mannon, president
Construction management professionals—estimators, superintendents, field engineers, project managers and construction managers—are the specialty of this local firm, in business since 1982. Makes permanent placements from Portland to Bellingham, from entry-level to executives. Pay range: $30,000-$100,000. Works on a contingency basis.

Cooper Personnel
1411 Fourth Ave., #1327
Seattle WA 98101
(206) 583-0722
Fax: (206) 223-4093
Contact: Bonnie Cooper
Established in 1988, this local firm has two specialties: administrative support and international trade, especially for those who speak Japanese or other Asian languages. The bilingual positions may be administrative, but there's an occasional management opportunity. A related degree and one to three years experience are helpful. Makes placements from Tacoma to Everett and on the Eastside. To apply, call for an appointment.

Corbett & Associates
1215 S. Central, #204-A
Kent WA 98032
(253) 854-1906
Fax: (253) 854-1485
http://www.corbettrecruiting.com
A local firm with clients across the U.S. in medical and pharmaceutical sales, sales management and marketing. These permanent usually require at least two or three years outside sales experience (although occasionally someone with 18 months experience can be considered). To inquire, you can call and then fax your resume. All fees employer paid.

The Coxe Group
1218 Third Ave., #1700
Seattle WA 98101-3021
(206) 467-4040
Fax: (206) 467-4038
http://www.coxegroup.com
consultants@coxegroup.com

Founded in Philadelphia in the 1970s and moved here in 1991, this consulting firm for architecture and engineering design offers executive search services. Most clients, however, are outside the Seattle area. Most positions require at least five or 10 years experience. If you submit a resume, it must be scannable. If you're using e-mail, a Microsoft Word document is preferred; it should be accompanied by a cover letter explaining your focus, your salary expectations and your willingness to relocate.

Cushman, Judith
See Judith Cushman & Associates

Egan, Kathi
See Kathi Egan Associates

Feldman Associates
3002 N.E. 87th
Seattle WA 98115
(206) 527-0980
Fax: (206) 527-1312
Contact: Renee Feldman
Specialty: sales, sales management and technical (operations, engineering) management positions in the chemical, industrial products, building products, plastics and packaging industries. Positions pay $50,000-$200,000. Most require several years experience and at least a B.A., usually in mechanical, chemical, manufacturing or industrial engineering. A local firm with national clients; about 40 per cent of the searches are for local jobs. Paid on a contingency basis. Founded in 1990.

F-O-R-T-U-N-E Personnel Consultants of East King County
11661 S.E. 1st St., #202
Bellevue WA 98005
(425) 450-9665
Fax: (425) 450-0357
fortuneseattle@seanet.com
Contact: Dan Chin, president
Industry focus: heavy manufacturing, including heavy equipment, mobile equipment and materials handling. Within these industries, fills engineering (electrical, mechanical and industrial), purchasing and sales management positions at the mid-management and higher levels. Works for national clients, but all positions are here. Paid on a contingency basis. Established in 1995.

Gordon Kamisar Esq. National Legal Search Consultants
1509 Queen Anne Ave. N., #298
Seattle WA 98109
(425) 392-1969
Fax: (425) 557-0080
http://www.seattlesearch.com
gkamisar@sprynet.com
Contact: Gordon Kamisar, Esq., principal
Attorneys for both private practice and corporate counsel is the specialty of this local firm founded in 1990. About 90 per cent of its placements are in the Seattle area. Many positions require three to six years experience in high tech; for

example, in intellectual property or securities. To contact the firm, submit a resume via fax or e-mail and follow up by mail. Works on a contingency basis.

Goto & Company

7981 168th Ave. N.E., #27
Redmond WA 98052
(425) 869-8092
Fax: (425) 881-9500
hiroshigoto@msn.com
Contact: Hiroshi Goto
Nearly all the clients for this local search firm are Japanese firms seeking staff for Northwest offices. Some positions are entry-level; others are supervisory or at the vice president level. Some candidates must be bilingual. All fees are employer paid. Resumes may be submitted by fax, mail or e-mail.

Hagel & Co.

1111 Third Ave., #2500
Seattle WA 98101
(206) 624-6674
success@hagel.net
Contact: Frank Hagel
Works on a retainer basis in Washington and Oregon in the public sector, for not-for-profits and in business, especially banking. Most searches involve positions at the director or higher level and require at least at least seven years of experience and a B.A. (with some clients preferring a graduate degree). Established in 1993. Accepts unsolicited resumes only by e-mail; retains only those resumes applicable to typical searches.

Hallmark Placements

1904 Third Ave., #819
Seattle WA 98101
(206) 587-5360
Fax: (206) 587-5319
Contact: Dolores Gohndrone, manager
Focus: temporary and permanent placements in engineering, food service (including bartenders, chefs and management) and administration (from clerks to accounting managers). Most positions pay $60,000 or less. Most engineering jobs require five to 10 years experience, most sales jobs three to five years similar experience and the most senior level accounting positions require at least five years experience. At the lower level, half of the fees are paid by the job-seeker; check when you apply. To apply, call for an appointment. Lower level positions require skills testing. Locally owned; founded in 1981.

Healthcare Specialists

400 108th Ave. N.E., #310
Bellevue WA 98004
Fax: (425) 454-6776
Contacts:
Deni Sutherland, recruiter: (425) 454-0678
Lisa Ward, recruiter: (425) 454-9313

Founded by Kathy Evans in 1976, this sales and sales management search firm now has new owners and a new name. The focus remains the same: outside sales and sales management for the medical, dental and pharmaceutical industries. For an entry-level position, you'll need at three to five years successful experience in outside sales and a degree (some employers also require a grade point average of at least 3.0). Many candidates come from sales jobs in consumer products, business products or the cellular industry. Such positions may pay $50,000 plus a car allowance. For higher level positions, employers prefer applicable industry experience (e.g., in the cardio-vascular field) and candidates with established contacts. Works on a contingency basis.

Helstrom Turner & Associates
10900 N.E. 8th St., #900
Bellevue WA 98004
(425) 868-1617
Fax: (425) 868-5385
htaseattle@aol.com
Contact: (Ms.) Kim Villeneuve, partner
Headquartered in Los Angeles, this woman-owned search firm specializes in the retail and restaurant industries. Only about five per cent of its searches are for positions in the Seattle area. Positions range from trend manager to CEO. Most require at least 10-15 years experience. Works on retainer. Particularly interested in women candidates with senior-level experience. To contact the firm, submit a resume (two pages maximum).

Hospitality Services Inc.
6625 S. 190th, #B-108
Kent WA 98032
(425) 251-1901
Fax: (425) 251-1903
Contact: Marvin Miller, president
Looking for a job with a restaurant, hotel, hospital, country club or with a caterer? This local firm makes temporary and permanent placements in positions ranging from busser to CEO, from Olympia to Bellingham. Most opportunities are in hotel front desk and sales positions and in restaurant management. At a minimum, candidates should have a stable work history (not five employers in five years, warns Marvin Miller), good customer service skills and a pleasant appearance. To apply, call for an interview. Also shares a North End office with:

Human Resources Inc.
10564 5th Ave. N.E., #204
Seattle WA 98125
(206) 368-9039
Fax: (206) 368-9243

Houser, Martin, Morris & Associates
P.O. Box 90015
Bellevue WA 98009
(425) 453-2700
Fax: (425) 453-8726
http://www.houser.com
Contact: Bob Holert, president
Established here in 1974; specializes in technical staff, managers and executives. Also handles executive director searches for trade associations and government agencies and attorney openings in private practices and corporations. Most openings require a B.A. (many a master's degree) and a minimum of three years experience. Works on both a contingency and retainer basis.

HR Services Inc.
1001 Fourth Ave., #3200
Seattle WA 98154
(206) 340-1471
Fax: (206) 340-0113
http://www.aa.net/hrservices
hrsvcs@aa.net
Contact: Victoria Cobos, president
Human resources positions (from recruiters, compensation specialist and benefits analysts to managers) on a temporary (three months or longer) and permanent basis are the specialty of this local firm established in 1988. Some part-time opportunities, both temporary and permanent. Most positions require four to seven years corporate (rather than employment agency) experience, a degree and CEBS or equivalent certification. Temporary assignments pay $14-$30 an hour, permanent positions $35,000-$75,000. All fees employer paid.

HRA Insurance Staffing
11100 N.E. 8th St., #600
Bellevue WA 98004
(425) 451-4007
Contact: Cindy Boe, managing partner
Specialty: permanent property casualty insurance positions along Puget Sound's Interstate 5 corridor. Even entry-level candidates should have at least a year of experience in an insurance company or brokerage. Established in 1986; locally owned. Works on a contingency basis.

Human Resource Alternatives
4040 Lake Washington Blvd., #105
Kirkland WA 98033
(425) 739-4300
Fax: (425) 739-7848
A division of CDI. Provides human resources professionals (HR specialist to director) on a contract (two or three months minimum) and permanent basis. Some positions become temp-to-perm. Typical pay is $25 an hour; a senior recruiter might make $40 an hour. Most positions require a degree and at least three years experience in human resources. To apply, submit a cover letter and resume; you'll

be interviewed if your skills match client needs. You may be interviewed faster if you've been referred by a client. All fees employer paid.

Humphrey Recruiting
P.O. Box 8067
Tacoma WA 98408
(253) 862-8806; from Bellevue: (425) 451-0330
Voice mail: (253) 474-8042
Fax: (253) 862-3689
Contact: Diann Humphrey, president
Thinking resorts, clubs, restaurants or hotels? This local firm specializes in mid-management and higher hospitality placements (including executive chef) in Washington, Oregon, Idaho, California and British Columbia. Positions pay a minimum of $30,000. Works with experienced candidates; a degree or specialized training is helpful. You'll also need a stable work history (candidates who are currently or were until recently employed are preferred) and a record of accomplishments. For example, a candidate for an executive chef position needs to demonstrate profitability.

Humphrey/Nelson Group
1420 Fifth Ave., #2200
Seattle WA 98101
(206) 224-2887
Fax: (206) 224-2880
Contacts: John Humphrey and Nena Nelson, principals
Established in 1997. Specializes in technical professionals, managers and salespeople and human resources staff, from receptionists to vice presidents. A candidate for a software engineering or programming job should have at least two years experience and a B.S.; technical managers and sales reps should have at least five years experience and a minimum of a bachelor's degree. HR manager-candidates should have at least five years experience and a B.A. To submit your credentials, call the Seattle office for a telephone screening.

Hurd Siegal & Associates
1111 Third Ave., #2880
Seattle WA 98101
(206) 622-4282
Fax: (206) 622-4058
hsiegal2@compuserve.com
Contact: Larry Siegal, principal
A local search firm established in 1991 that does about 25 per cent of its placements in the Seattle area. Focus: senior management (directors and above) for manufacturing and distribution companies. If you submit a resume, it'll be kept on file for a year.

Insurance Overload Systems
19515 North Creek Parkway, #314
Bothell WA 98011
(425) 806-3971
Fax: (425) 806-3972
Contact: (Ms.) Kelly Lynch, branch manager

Headquartered in Dallas with an office here since 1994. Specialty: the insurance industry (life, health, property, casualty, for brokerage firms, agencies and corporate worker's compensation programs), in positions ranging from clerks to manager. Places on a temporary (25 per cent of the business) and temp-to-perm basis. Candidates should have industry experience—a year for entry-level positions, at least three to five years for higher level jobs. To apply, call for a telephone interview; qualified candidates will be asked to fax in their resumes and schedule in-person interviews.

Insurance Staffing Inc.
2200 Sixth Ave., #407
Seattle WA 98121
(206) 728-1404
Fax: (206) 728-1406
insstaff@juno.com
Contacts: Eileen Lewis and Patricia Orozco-Daly
Established in 1995, this local firm files insurance industry positions from file clerks to department managers. Most positions pay less than $50,000. An entry-level position requires a career orientation, high energy level, good customer service skills and proficiency with Microsoft Office and other basic office software. You should be able to keyboard 50 words per minute. A degree is important, but not mandatory for lower-level jobs. To apply, call for an interview; allow at least 90 minutes for your screening and tests.

Intelligent Life
3513 N.E. 45th St., Mezzanine Level
Seattle WA 98105
(206) 812-0786
Fax: (206) 812-0793
http://www.int-life.com
info@int-life.com
Contact: Beryl Gorbman
Locally owned, this firm focuses on new media: for example, web site developers, audio/video editors, digital media, audio mixers, video and film production and computer graphics. At a minimum, candidates should have a year or two of relevant experience. Degrees are helpful. To apply, watch for newspaper or web site ads for the type of job you seek.

Jones Consulting Group
1335 N. Northlake Way, #101
Seattle WA 98103
(206) 548-0109
Fax: (206) 545-8339
jones_search_partners@msn.com
Contact: Janet Jones, principal
Specialties: consumer packaged goods (especially wine) and construction management (both commercial and production residential), usually for positions paying at least $100,000 and requiring more than eight years experience. If your background matches the kind of searches the firm typically does, you can mail in (not fax) a resume that'll be filed for a year. Works on a retainer basis.

Judith Cushman & Associates

1125 12th Ave. N.W., #B-1A
Issaquah WA 98027
(425) 392-8660
Fax: (425) 391-9190
http://www.jc-a.com
info@jc-a.com
Contact: Judith Cushman, president
A locally owned firm that specializes in mid to senior level marketing communications including public relations and investor relations positions. National and local clients. Emphasis in high technology. Works on a retainer basis. For marketing communications professionals with fewer than five years experience, has established The Recruiting Connection.

Kamisar, Gordon

See Gordon Kamisar Esq. National Legal Search Consultants

Kathi Egan Associates

2611 N.E. 125th St., #204
Seattle WA 98125
(206) 361-4802
Contact: Kathi Egan
This search firm does not accept unsolicited resumes but will consider calls from qualified candidates. Focus: property casualty insurance, for positions that require at least three to five years experience. Works in Washington, Oregon, northern Idaho and Alaska on a contingency basis.

Lacasse Maritime Crew Service

2500 Westlake Ave. N., #K
Seattle WA 98109
(206) 282-1330
Fax: (206) 378-1338
Contact: Beverly Lacasse
Places crews on luxury yachts all over the U.S.—captains, mates, engineers, stewards, deckhands and housekeepers. Work is full-time permanent; a year's commitment is required. Limited opportunities in the Seattle area.

Lakeside Personnel

1818 Westlake Ave. N., #126
Seattle WA 98109
(206) 284-6066
Fax: (206) 282-8289
Contacts:
Sig Bergquist, president
Ed M. Lee, retail recruitment specialist
Specialty: retail—from trainee to mid-management, in positions paying $22,000-$45,000. Most jobs are at the store-level along the Interstate 5 corridor. Most require retail experience; a degree is helpful. Resumes are accepted by mail and fax.

Law Dawgs

1201 Third Ave., #2810
Seattle WA 98101
(206) 224-8244
Fax: (206) 224-8291
http://www.jetcity.com/~lawdawgs.html
lawdawgs@jetcity.com
Contact: Ewen Cameron, president
Places legal professionals, including paralegals and contract attorneys, on a temporary, temp-to-hire and permanent basis in law firms and corporations. Some attorneys work as long as eight months on contract; some are hired after working on contract. A local firm established in 1995. To apply, call for more information; applicants are screened prior to being interviewed. All fees employer paid.

Management Recruiters International

9725 S.E. 36th, #312
Mercer Island WA 98040
(206) 232-0204
http://www.mrinet.com
mercer!@mrinet.com
Contact: Jim Dykeman, president
A franchise, this firm specializes in placements in the electrical connector, Internet software, sports apparel and pharmaceutical and nutrition industries. Level: mid to senior management, including design engineers, sales reps and sales managers, shoe designers and scientists. Salaries range from $45,000 to $150,000. About 10 per cent of the positions are local. Works on a contingency basis.

Management Recruiters International

10900 N.E. Fourth St., #1450
Bellevue WA 98004
(425) 462-5104
Fax: (425) 462-1614
http://www.mrinet.com
Contact: Isaac Menda, manager
Focus: attorneys and paralegals for the securities industry. Works on a contingency basis.

Management Recruiters of Lynnwood

19109 36th W., #100
Lynnwood WA 98036
(425) 778-1212
Fax: (425) 778-7840
lynwood!bud@mrinet.com
Contact: Bud Naff, general manager
This franchise, established in 1988, specializes in permanent placements in environmental consulting and engineering, construction (for example, estimators and construction managers), civil engineering design (for example, airports, tunnels, wastewater facilities) and diagnostic imaging in health care (both hands-on professionals and managers in CAD, CT, MRI and ultrasound). Salary range: $30,000 and above. Works on a contingency basis.

Management Recruiters of Tacoma

2709 Jahn Ave. N.W.
Gig Harbor WA 98335
(253) 858-9991, (800) 863-1872
Fax: (253) 858-5140
Contact: Dennis Johnson, manager
This franchise specializes in permanent placements in medicine (doctors, nurses and therapists), health care management (usually requires a degree and at least five to 10 years of managemet experience), high technology (including software developers and project managers) and accounting and finance (controller and more senior positions). Most placements pay $50,000 or more. All fees employer paid.

Maritime Employment Services Inc.

74 S. Lucille
Seattle WA 98134
(206) 767-5180
Fax: (206) 767-5288
http://www.maritimemployment.com
jobs@maritimemployment.com
Founded in 1988, this local firm places crews (factory to licensed wheelhouse staff) on fishing, deep sea, cruise, casino and towing vessels. Temporary (perhaps just a few weeks) and permanent. Fees are paid by job applicants. To apply, call for an appointment.

Maritime Recruiters

P.O. Box 260
Mercer Island WA 98040
(206) 232-6041
Fax: (206) 232-6041
Contact: Bob Walton, senior partner
Since 1969, making permanent (90 per cent of the business) and contract placements in the maritime industry. Only about 10 per cent of the jobs are sea-going; others may be in naval architecture, admiralty law, engineering, design of marine machinery, operations, off-shore oil drilling, shipyard management and trades, finance, marine insurance and translation (Russian, Japanese and Chinese). Most positions require at least five years experience. To apply, submit a resume (reverse chronological format). If your background matches the firm's current needs, you'll be screened by telephone. All fees employer paid.

McIntire & Carr

P.O. Box 1176
Issaquah WA 98027
(425) 391-9320
Fax:(425) 557-7943
mlm@halcyon.com
Contact: Merlin McIntire
Focus: sales and sales management and product management of such products as medical and industrial equipment, pharmaceuticals, software, office products, printing and telecommunications. Seventy-five per cent of the jobs are in Seattle or Portland. Candidates should have two to five years documented success in

outside sales and a degree; for junior positions in pharmaceuticals, some employers even require a certain grade point average. Pay: $30,000-$65,000 plus incentive. All fees employer paid.

McKain Consulting
600 First Ave., #617
Seattle WA 98104
(206) 749-0694
Fax:(206) 749-0695
bmckain@juno.com
Contact: Brian McKain, principal
Focus: permanent positions (senior professionals and mid to senior management) in consulting engineering and environmental consulting. Most pay at least $60,000. Only about 15 per cent of the placements are local. Works on a retainer basis. A local firm established in 1992.

Medic-Focus
2121 Westlake Ave. N., #401
Seattle WA 98109-2448
(206) 285-6955
Fax: (206) 285-3425
eboisen@aol.com
Contact: Elliott G. Boisen, M.D.
Since 1994, this local search firm has placed doctors in patient care and management positions, administrators, nurse practioners and physician assistants. Most placements are local. All fees employer paid.

Medzilla/The Franklin Search Group
14522 54th Pl. W.
Edmonds WA 98020
(425) 742-4292
Fax:(425) 742-2172
http://www.medzilla.com
info@medzilla.com
Contact: Frank Heasley
Clinical research, regulatory affairs, fermentation and data management are the areas where this search firm needed candidates most in late 1997. Specializing in high technology, health care and biotechnology, usually on a permanent basis, it places physicians, post-docs, programmers, research associates, managers and vice presidents. Jobs require at least a B.A. (in many cases, a graduate degree) and may start as low as $35,000. Most pay $50,000 or more. Many require relocation. Works on a retainer or contingency basis.

Meyer Enterprises Counselors & Consultants
3428 85th Dr. S.E.
Everett WA 98205
(425) 335-0900
Fax: (425) 334-9192
whatnow@halcyon.com
Contact: Chaz Meyer
Most of this firm's local business is in electrical and mechanical engineering

positions; most require five or more years experience and pay $35,000-$85,000. Also places insurance professionals and managers, but usually in California. Local firm, established in 1987. All fees employer paid.

Millennium Staffing

601 Union St., #1625
Seattle WA 98101
(206) 464-4055
Fax: (206) 464-4147
millennium@seanet.com
Contact: Steve Curran, staffing consultant
Part of a national launched in 1997; affiliated with Accountants On Call. Provides project and permanent placement of "administrative and creative services professionals" for web-site and desktop publishing creation and higher-level administrative support. Candidates need to be able to communicate well and have strong software and creative skills. How to approach: send in your resume first; the most qualified candidates will be interviewed.

Miller & Miller Executive Search

P.O. Box 3088
Kirkland WA 98083
(425) 827-9194
Fax: (425) 822-3145
Focus: management and occasional clinical positions (for example, discovery research) in biotechnology and biomedicine. Locally owned; founded in 1989.

Minzel & Associates

1191 Second Ave., #1900
Seattle WA 98101
(206) 689-8526
Fax: (206) 628-9506
m-and-a@msn.com
Contact: Jeff Minzel
Provides attorneys and paralegals on a temporary and temp-to-hire basis to government agencies, law firms and corporations. To apply, fax your resume; if your background meets the firm's current needs, you'll be interviewed.

Moore Recruiting Group

6947 Coal Creek Pkwy S.E., #266
Newcastle WA 98056
(425) 369-7208
Fax: (425) 271-6436
mrg@halcyon.com
Contact: Bob Moore
A local search firm specializing in insurance, including adjusters and sales and marketing positions, and high technology, including MIS staff, programmers, software developers, systems administrators and sales and marketing positions. At a minimum, candidates need a B.A. and three to five years experience. Works on a contingency basis.

Moss & Co.

12145 Arrow Point Loop N.E.
Bainbridge Island WA 98110
(206) 842-4035
Contact: Barbara Moss
Real estate development and construction, including such positions as property manager, geotechnical engineer and contractor, are the focus of this local firm, which is paid on an hourly basis by employers. Most of the placements are local; most require at least five years experience and a degree. If your background matches the firm's usual requirements, your resume will be kept on file. Founded in 1989.

The Oldani Group

188 106th Ave. N.E., #420
Bellevue WA 98004
(425) 451-3938
Fax: (425) 453-6786
http://www.theoldanigroup.com
searches@theoldanigroup.com
Contact: Jerry Oldani, principal
A local search firm specializing in executive level public sector positions (directors and above for ports and counties, typically paying at least $60,000) and, effective spring, 1998, on executive level private sector jobs. Works on retainer.

Personnel Consultants

14042 N.E. 8th, #201-B
Bellevue WA 98007
(425) 641-0657
Fax: (425) 641-0657
buzy73A@prodigy.com
Contact: Larry Dykes, recruiter
Specialty: the insurance industry, including positions in claims, risk management, actuarial, underwriting and sales and marketing for brokers and carriers. Both temporary (often several months) and permanent placements. Most positions require six or more years industry experience. All fees employer paid.

Power Conversion International

120 W. Dayton, #B-6
Edmonds WA 98020
(425) 771-3373
Fax: (425) 771-3204
Contact: Gary Carter, principal
Headquartered here since 1989, but makes only about five per cent of its placements in this area. Focus: a wide range of functions within the power supply industry. Typical opportunities require at least four to seven years experience; only occasional entry-level positions. Fees are employer paid.

Premiere Search
25025 S.E. Klahanie Blvd., #G-205
Issaquah WA 98029
(425) 313-5099
Fax: (425) 557-3778
premiersearch@prostar.com
Contact: Richard Hugill, president
Focus: corporate franchise management positions, including operations and franchise sales. Most clients are national. Most positions require five to 10 years experience in a functional specialty or in franchising. Typical base compensation: $50,000-$70,000 in sales positions, $60,000-$80,000 in operations. Works on a contingency basis.

PRN MedSearch
209 E. 4th Ave., #204
Olympia WA 98501
(360) 754-4423
FAx: (360) 754-4426
http://www.halycon.com/prnmed/
prnmed@halcyon.com
Contact: Al Todak, medical recruiter
Focus: medical professionals (for example, doctors) and executives. Because Washington is a "buyers' market" for doctors, most of this firm's placements are outside the area. Works on a contingency basis.

Public Schools Personnel Cooperative
601 McPhee Rd. S.W.
Olympia WA 98502
(360) 753-2855
Jobline: (360) 664-2058
Substitute service (certified): (360) 753-3270
Substitute services (classified): (360) 753-2855
Fax: (360) 664-2057
http://www.esd113.wednet.edu/personnel/
Contact: Laura Barckley, director
Posts openings and accepts applications for Educational Service District 113; for certified (teaching) positions in 11 south Puget Sound school districts; and for classified (support and technical) jobs in four of the same districts . Interviews are scheduled and conducted by districts with openings. The job application form is online, although you must print it out and mail it in with other materials (such as proof of certification).

Pursuant Legal Consultants Attorney Placement
P.O. Box 2347
Seattle WA 98119
(206) 682-2599
Contact: Allen G. Norman, principal
Founded in New York in 1984 and relocated here in 1996, this search firm places attorneys in law firms (about a third of the firm's business) and in corporations. At least half of the firm's clients are in Seattle and Portland. Most opportunities require two to seven years experience and admission to the appropriate state's bar.

Depending on current trends, may seek candidates with experience in environmental law, intellectual property or tax. To submit your credentials, mail in a cover letter that describes your background and goals along with a resume (two pages maximum). Candidates who match the firm's usual needs will be contacted. Most work is on a retainer basis.

R.A. Ward & Associates
203 Bellevue Way N.E., #492
Bellevue WA 98004
(800) 639-8127
Fax: (206) 727-5194
http://www.raward.com
info@raward.com
A search firm that specializes in health care and information technology. Seldom has searches in the Seattle area. Works on a contingency basis.

The Recruiting Connection
1125 12th Ave. N.W., #B-1A
Issaquah WA 98027
(425) 392-8660
Fax: (425) 391-9190
http://www.jc-a.com
info@jc-a.com
Affiliated with Judith Cushman & Associates. Provides an employer-paid placement service for more junior marketing communications professionals (including public relations and investor relations), typically those with fewer than five years experience. Typical positions pay less than $55,000. See web site for submission information.

Resource Management Services
1501 Fourth Ave., #450
Seattle WA 98101
(206) 223-8991
Fax: (206) 223-8227
resourcemgt@msn.com
Contact: Suzanne Coleman, executive administrator
Affiliated with Parker Services. Places technical professionals and managers on an interim and permanent basis in such service orgaizations as health care, retail, financial services and hospitality (including web site designers, network administrators and content developers). Most positions require a degree and at least five years experience. Salary range: $35,000-$85,000. All fees employer paid.

Richards Williams & Associates
(425) 672-3260
Fax: (425) 334-9065
rwa@seanet.com
Focus: human resources management jobs for Silicon Valley clients. Only about five per cent of the firm's searches are for jobs in Washington and Oregon. Most require three to five years experience and pay $65,000-$130,000. Address withheld upon request.

Roth Young Executive Search of Seattle
305 111th Ave. N.E.
Bellevue WA 98004
(425) 455-2141
Fax: (425) 455-0067
Contact: Dave Salzberg, president
A licensee of a national firm; opened its office here in 1967. Does 50 per cent of its searches for Washington, Oregon and Alaska jobs. Works on both retainer and contingency. Focus: mid-management and higher positions in manufacturing, food processing, the beverage and juice industries and hospitality. May also place sales and marketing staff, from sales reps to vice presidents, in food, consumer products, industrial, telecommunications and high tech industries.

Russell A. Lager & Associates
P.O. Box 60111
Seattle WA 98160
(206) 448-2616
Contact: Russell A. Lager, principal
A local firm that conducts searches in the western U.S. About 65 per cent of its searches are for Seattle-area positions. Established in 1981. Focus: sales and marketing positions in consumer packaged goods and food service (sales to restaurants and institutions). Prefers candidates with at least five years experience in consumer packaged goods. Typical base compensation: $48,000-$80,000.

Sea People
4005 20th Ave. W.
Seattle WA 98199
(206) 283-6595
Fax: (206) 283-6395
Contact: Michelle Gray
Specialty: temporary, contract and permanent positions in commercial fishing (80 per cent of the business) and such other maritime work as tugs and charters. Positions range from captains, mates and engineers to factory jobs, deckhands and land-based cooks. Occasional entry-level opportunities. Candidates can walk in or mail a resume. Most fees are paid by job-seekers.

Sheridan Company
603 Stewart St., #405
Seattle WA 98101
(206) 682-3773
Fax: (206) 682-8466
Contact: Thomas Jobe, consultant
Focus: financial services, including commercial banking, credit, international banking, international trade and sales and marketing of financial services. About 60 per cent of the positions are here, about 20 per cent in Portland. Most postions require at least two to three years of related experience and a degree in business, finance, accounting or international business. For international banking or trade, bilingual candidates are more easily placed (Japanese or Chinese). Locally owned. Most work is on a contingency basis. Resumes (two pages maximum) can be mailed or faxed.

Strategic Resources Group
1697 116th Ave. N.E., #104
Bellevue WA 98004
(425) 688-1151
Fax: (425) 688-1272
http://www.strategicresources.com
info@strategicresources.com
Contact: Philip Kagan, president
Organized in 1990, this is a boutique of separate recruiters operating together. Each has different specialties: animal health and nutrition and food sciences, animal health sales and marketing; advertising; environmental engineering; apparel manufacturing and design; senior finance executives; ethnic marketing; and corporate security. Many searches are for positions outside this area. Most jobs require at least three to five years experience and, for the sciences, often a graduate degree. Some engineering jobs require a P.E. Most pay a minimum of $50,000. Resumes can be submitted by mail, fax or e-mail; those that match the firm's needs are permanently filed on CD-ROM. Works primarily on a contingency basis.

Susan Clevenger Executive Search
2535 152nd Ave. N.E., #A
Redmond WA 98052
(425) 885-7666
Fax: (425) 869-9378
Contact: Susan Clevenger, principal
Focus: mid-range professionals and senior managers in such fields as geotechnical, property management, finance, insurance, sales and professional services. No high tech jobs or clients. Most searches involve jobs requiring at least five years experience and paying a base of at least $75,000. Candidates can mail resumes (two pages maximum) and cover letters indicating salary requirements and willingness to relocate. All fees employer paid on an hourly, contingency or retainer basis.

Svei Hagel & Co.
P.O. Box 16484
Seattle WA 98116
(206) 935-9630
Only about 20 per cent of this firm's work is done in the Puget Sound area, in such industries as transportation and utilities, both public and private sector. Most searches require candidates with at least seven to 10 years of experience and a bachelor's degree. Most positions are at the director or higher level. Established in 1987. Does not accept unsolicited resumes.

The Thomas Co.
5434 S.E. 167th Pl.
Renton WA 98058
(425) 255-7637
Contact: Thomas Yankowski, executive director
Health care management (rather than clinical) and insurance positions ae the specialty of this local search firm established in 1979. Positions pay at least $40,000. About a quarter of the opportunities are local. If your experience matches the firm's focus, you can mail in a resume. Those relevant to typical searches will be kept on file. All fees employer paid.

Thomas & Associates
3221 26th Ave. W.
Seattle WA 98199
(206) 283-9246
jthomas@aol.com
Contact: Jim Thomas, principal
Specialty: both clinical (doctors and nurses, for example) and management (including human resources and operations directors and CFOs) staff for health care providers (hospitals and medical groups) in several Northwestern states (including Alaska). About 30 per cent of the opportunities are in the Seattle area. Most business-side positions require five to 10 years experience and a graduate degree. How many opportunities locally are there for doctors? Depends on the specialty. For a family practitioner, for example, positions typically pay $100,000 or more. A local firm established in 1988.

Thomson, Sponar & Adams (TSA, Inc.)
10116 36th Ave. Ct. S.W., #200
Lakewood WA 98499
(253) 588-1216
Fax: (253) 588-2528
http://www.aaa-mall.com/tsa/
tsa@frugal.com
Contact: Frank Adams, president
Specialty: technical professionals and managers (to CEOs) for start-ups as well as large firms in such fields as high energy physics, applied superconductivity, gas and communications, materials, computer hardware and software. At press time, the firm's searches included chemical, mechanical and cryogenics engineers, with such positions requiring either a B.S. and at least five years experience or a graduate degree and two to five years experience. All fees employer paid.

Visionaries Sports & Entertainment Corp.
114 1/2 1st Ave. S.
Seattle WA 98104
(206) 224-9313
Fax: (206) 224-9315
newpicasso@aol.com
Contact: Rick Edwards, CEO
A local firm established in the early 1990s. Focus: experienced professionals and managers (including designers and product development and marketing staff) for sports gear manufacturers and entertainment firms. Most positions require five to 10 years experience. All fees employer paid.

Waldron & Company
101 Stewart St., #1200
Seattle WA 98101
(206) 441-4144
Fax: (206) 441-5213
Contact: Tom Waldron, president
Handles management positions in the public sector and nonprofits. Most searches

involve positions requiring at least five years experience. Affiliated with an interim placement firm and a career search assistance firm.

State of Washington
Department of Personnel
600 S. Franklin
Olympia WA 98504
http://www.wa.gov.DOP
The state maintains its own executive search agency, which also handles searches on a fee basis for local government. It also has a special office for mid-management positions. Like other search consultants, these offices do not encourage unsolicited resumes.

Executive Search Services
Washington State Department of Personnel
600 S. Franklin
P.O. Box 47530
Olympia WA 98504-7530
(360) 664-0394
Fax: (360) 586-1369
http://www.wa.gov/DOP/employ.html
Since 1992 this small office has served as the state's in-house executive recruiter, identifying candidates for positions as directors, deputy directors and assistant directors. Also conducts searches for city and county agencies. It is the U.S.'s only state-operated search agency. Most positions pay $50,000-$100,000.

Washington Management Service
521 Capitol Way S.
Box 47500
(360) 753-2303
Jobline: (360) 753-5368
Skills bank: (360) 753-2302
http://www.wa.gov/DOP/lib/general/wms.text
Established in 1994 to help individual agencies fill mid-management positions. Operates a clearinghouse for state agencies seeking managers, state employees considering job changes and private-sector managers considering government service. Covers 3,500 positions. The web site lists departments that have five or more WMS jobs and encourages candidates to contact these agencies directly.

8. Employment Agencies

Looking for a secretarial position? You're a dental assistant, a paralegal, a teacher, a medical bookkeeper? Want an entry-level help desk stint, clerical assignment or warehouse work? These are examples of the positions handled by the firms listed in this chapter. Because many of these employment agencies also handle other job functions or professional-level positions, you may also find the firms listed in other chapters.

In general, there are three kinds of opportunities available through employment agencies. Temporary assignments can be as short as four hours; you may be filling in for vacationing or ill employees or assisting with rush work or a special project. Temps are paid by the employment agency.

"Temp-to-hire," sometimes called "temp-to-perm," means that you start work on a temporary basis with the understanding that you might later be transferred to a permanent position on the employer's payroll. This "conversion" may take place in as little as 40 hours; some agencies ask employers to make a decision after 520 hours. Whether the transfer takes place may depend on how well you do your job and fit into the company—or whether the the employer sees a need for (and can afford) another position.

Finally, employment agencies also make permanent or direct placements. In this situation, the agency serves as an extension of the employer's personnel function, often advertising an opening, testing and screening candidates and then recommending a few top candidates to the employer for interviews.

How do employment agencies get paid? When a temp is placed, the agency is compensated by the difference between what it charges the employer (say, $10 an hour) and what it pays the temp ($8 an hour, perhaps). Some agencies charge a conversion fee when a temporary is transferred to the employer's payroll. This fee is usually paid by the employer. With permanent placements, the agency often is paid a fee—usually by the employer, but occasionally by the candidate—based on the salary for the position.

Besides traditional employment agencies, this chapter includes examples of personnel co-ops, in-house government temp agencies and other placement services.

Able & Associates
2314 E. Union, #204
Seattle WA 98122
(206) 860-0019
Fax: (206) 860-1390
Contact: Joyce Jones, office manager
This locally-owned employment agency offers temporary and permanent placement in technical (including civil, chemical and software engineering, technical writing and free-lance writing), clerical and light industrial jobs. You can register at either the Seattle or Tacoma office. Candidates should have a stable work history (a minimum of one to three years preferred) and, especially for clerical positions,

expertise with such software programs as Microsoft Office, Quicken, QuickBooks and Peachtree accounting. (Tip: When you go to register, dress as you would for an interview.)

Accountants Inc.
500 108th N.E., #2350
Bellevue WA 98004
(425) 454-4111
Fax: (425) 454-4906
http://www.accountantsinc.com
bellevue@accountantsinc.com
Contact: Elizabeth Look, branch manager
Specializes in temporary (one day to one year) and permanent placement in accounting and finance. Two local offices; all fees employer-paid. Positions range from accounting clerk to CFO and finance director. Candidates should have a stable work history; a B.A. is sufficient for many positions, but you'll need a CPA for the top accounting jobs and an MBA for many finance opportunities. (Tip: you'll have a better chance at the best jobs if you have a well-prepared resume and if you can present yourself well in person.)

Accountants Inc.
1420 Fifth Ave., #1711
Seattle WA 98101
(206) 621-0111
Fax: (206) 621-0285
http://www.accountantsinc.com
mrefvem@accountantsinc.com
Contact: Mary Refvem, branch manager

Accountants Northwest
520 Pike St., #2605
Seattle WA 98101
(206) 269-1133
Fax: (206) 441-6344
http://www.ntss.com
Part of Northwest Temporary Services, a local firm. Offers temporary, temporary-to-hire and permanent placement in accounting positions ranging from clerks to accounts receivable to controller.

Accountants On Call
601 Union St., #1625
Seattle WA 98101
(206) 467-0700
Fax: (206) 467-9986
http://www.aocnet.com
Affiliated with Accountants Executive Search. Handles temporary, temp-to-hire and permanent placements in accounting and finance jobs paying less than $30,000. In late 1997, estimated that a staff accountant working on a temporary basis could make $12.50-$15 an hour, a financial analyst $12-$16 and an experienced controller with CPA $18-$40. In most cases, jobs require a degree, a minimum of one to three years experience and excellent Excel skills.

Accountemps
601 Union St., #4300
Seattle WA 98101
(206) 749-9161
Fax: (206) 749-9243
http://www.accountemps.com
seattle@accountemps.com
Part of Robert Half International. Offers temporary placements in accounting and
finance. In late 1997, was filling such positions as interim controller, accounting
manager and Securities and Exchange Commission (SEC) specialist.

Accountemps
10900 N.E. 4th, #1650
Bellevue WA 98004
(425) 451-1000
Fax: (425) 455-1898
http://www.accountemps.com
bellevue@accountemps.com

Accountemps
2505 S. 320th St., #120
Federal Way WA 98003
(253) 946-1776
Fax: (253) 946-2095
federalway@accountemps.com

Accountemps
3400 188th St. S.W., #165
Lynnwood WA 98037
(425) 712-7166
Does not accept unsolicited resumes by fax.

Accounting Partners
500 108th Ave. N.E., #1640
Bellevue WA 98004
(425) 450-1990
Fax: (425) 450-1056
http:/www.apartner.com
Specializes in accounting and finance, doing both temporary and permanent
placements. Positions range from accounting clerk to controller, from data entry to
financial analyst. Most upper level accounting positions are for staff accountants;
you should have an accounting degree and one to three years experience. A CPA
is an excellent credential, but not as important as the appropriate experience. Such
positions pay $11-$15 an hour. A financial analyst should have at least two years
experience; a degree is preferred. You'll also need proficiency with a spreadsheet
management program. Almost all jobs require DOS or Windows. A junior analyst
might make $10-$12 an hour, a more senior person $15-$25.

Accounting Quest

101 Stewart St., #1000
Seattle WA 98101
(206) 441-5600
Fax: (206) 441-5656
gregg@accountingquest.com
Contact: Greg Gillard, office director
Specialty: temporary and permanent positions in accounting and finance for high-technology and high-growth companies between Tacoma and Everett. Also offices in Portland and Denver. Positions range from accounting clerk to accounting manager, which might pay $40,000-$50,000, and controller, which might pay $50,000-$80,000; to senior financial analysts and finance directors, which might pay $40,000-$90,000; and to MIS systems implementation jobs, which might pay $35,000-$90,000. Lower-level positions require accounting education or fast data entry and a stable work history; for all positions, you'll need good references, evidence of progressively more responsible professional growth, a can-do attitude and enthusiasm. To apply, call or submit a resume (two pages maximum). Works on a contingency basis with all fees employer-paid.

Act Media

11807 North Creek Pkwy., #111
Bothell WA 98011
(425) 487-6792
Fax: (425) 487-6797
Ever wondered how people get hired to pass out coupons and samples in stores? This is one of the agencies that places "in-store representatives" in grocery and drug retailers. Shifts range from three to eight hours. Assignments almost always include weekends. Many workers are retirees or homemakers. Qualifications: an outgoing personality with a sales attitude, the ability to stand for several hours, reliable transportation and a neat appearance.

Adams & Associates

701 Fifth Ave., #3700
Seattle WA 98104
(206) 447-9200
http://www.adamsandassoc.com
Executive search: search@adamsandassoc.com
OSD: banomyongp@adamsandassoc.com
Adams Temporaries: gustafsonc@adamsandassoc.com
This locally owned firm has three divisions: executive search, for positions paying $55,000 and more; office support (OSD), for permanent placements in administrative support; and Adams Temporaries, for temporary and temp-to-hire placements. Typical executive search placements are for controllers, account executives, regional sales managers and marketing managers. Most require at least three to five years experience, a degree and documented success in previous positions. For OSD, recruiters prefer a stable work history (three to five years experience in your last job, unless you have excellent experience and exceptional references from jobs that lasted only a year or two), a commitment to the new job, outgoing personality, proficiency with Microsoft Office and the ability to keyboard 55-60 words per minute. All temporary positions in this office are clerical. Applicants for tempo-

rary positions may not need the same level of skills, but those with good skills are more likely to see their positions become permanent. All temporary applicants are tested. All fees employer paid.

Adams & Associates
16400 Southcenter Parkway, #400
Tukwila WA 98188
(206) 575-6266
Fax: (206) 575-6299
http://www.adamsandassoc.com
This office also places temporary workers in light industrial positions.

Adams & Associates
10900 N.E. 4th, #750
Bellevue WA 98004
(425) 454-5082
Fax: (425) 646-8860
http://www.adamsandassoc.com
This office also places temporary workers in light industrial positions.

Adecco Employment Services
701 Fifth Ave., #4630
Seattle WA 98104
(206) 587-3929
Fax: (206) 587-6560
http://www.adecco.com
jana.shook@adecco.com
Part of an international firm, this employment agency (formerly ADIA) provides temporary, temp-to-perm and permanent placements in administrative support, computer technology (for example, help desk), inside and outside sales and light industrial. Three offices: you can register at one and work from all. Candidates need a stable work history (two or three years is preferred), references and, except for industrial jobs, a "dressy casual corporate" appearance. Most jobs require expertise in Microsoft Word, Excel and Power Point and the ability to keyboard 50 words per minute. Average minimum pay: $8 per hour. All fees employer paid. How to apply: call first to schedule an interview and testing (allow two hours). Your references will be checked before you're sent out on any jobs. All fees employer paid.

Adecco Employment Services
550 Kirkland Way, #217
Kirkland WA 98033
(425) 739-2029
Fax: (425) 739-2225
Contact: Sherrill Lane, manager

Adecco Employment Services
3680 S. Cedar St., #H
Tacoma WA 98409
(253) 475-1500
Fax: (253) 475-3710
Contact: Paige Mead, manager

Adecco Employment Services
701 Fifth Ave., #4630
Seattle WA 98104
(206) 587-3929
Fax: (206) 587-6560
Contact: Mari Rogers, manager
The Kent branch opened in late 1997 will operate from the Seattle facility until space is located in 1998.

The Affiliates
601 Union St., #4300
Seattle WA 98101
(206) 749-9460
Fax: (206) 749-9243
Part of Robert Half International. Provides temporary and permanent placement of legal support staff, including paralegals.

Allied Forces/Labor Express
2834 Sunset Blvd. N.E.
Renton WA 98056
(425) 226-8080
Fax: (425) 226-9254
Offers daily pay for general labor (for example, residential construction) and technical and warehouse work. Offers temporary and temp-to-hire positions. You can walk in to apply between 6 a.m. and 4 p.m. weekdays. You must have valid picture identification to apply. A branch of an Arizona-headquartered firm; opened in 1996. Affiliated with:

Labor Express
419 Rainier Ave. S.
Seattle WA 98144
(206) 328-7307
Fax: (206) 328-7212
Opened in 1997 to handle only construction jobs. Offers daily pay for general labor (for example, demolition or construction clean-up). Temporary and temp-to-hire positions. You can apply by walking in between 6 a.m. and 4 p.m. weekdays; you'll need valid picture identification.

Allied Personnel Services

14900 Interurban Ave. S., #271
Seattle WA 98168
(206) 674-4563
Fax: (206) 674-4568
rnebeker@seanet.com
Contact: Robert Nebeker, president
A local firm established in 1995. Offers entry-level to experienced professionals on a contract and permanent basis in engineering (electrical, mechanical, structural and civil) and related technical fields (drafters, programmers and analysts, but no technical writers or graphic designers). All fees employer-paid. How to apply: call first and then send your resume.

Alternative Resource Corp.

2001 Sixth Ave., #2100
Seattle WA 98121
(206) 441-9772
Fax: (206) 441-3431
http://www.alrc.com
Contact: Diana Smith, branch manager
Headquartered in Illinois. Provides technical resources to information technology companies in such areas as connectivity support, desktop computing, help desk, Internet/intranet, mainframe/midrange and voice and data communications.

Almond & Associates

P.O. Box 6124
Federal Way WA 98063-6124
(253) 952-5555; from Seattle: (206) 721-1111
Fax: (253) 952-5560
This local firm provides executive search and also fills administrative support positions on a temporary, temp-to-hire and permanent basis; candidates need experience and excellent computer skills. All fees employer paid.

Anchor Staffing

160 N.W. Gilman Blvd., #3
Issaquah WA 98027
(425) 837-1355
Fax: (425) 837-1715
anchor_sr@msn.com
Contact: Pamela Gotham, principal
Established in 1995, this local firm provides executive search for interim and permanent positions in sales, technology, manufacturing and accounting. The agency also offers temporary and permanent placement in medical and health professions, entry-level to experienced. Typical positions: RNs, CNAs, physical therapists, speech pathologists and nurse practitioners. A third division offers placements in clerical and light industrial positions. All fees are employer-paid. To apply, you can call, write or e-mail; your resume (scannable, maximum two pages) will be filed for a year.

Another Source

4800 S. 188th St., #340
Seattle WA 98188
(206) 241-8906
Fax: (206) 241-2551
asource@sprynet.com

A personnel service, which screens applications received by its client companies, interviews the most qualified candidates and makes recommendations on which candidates should be interviewed by the client. All positions are permanent; most pay less than $40,000. They range from administrative support (including executive assistant), accounting (including supervisors and an occasional controller position), bookkeeping (including full-charge), human resources (including directors), inside telephone sales and customer service (including help desk). About half of the positions require degrees. All fees employer paid. Unsolicited resumes (two pages maximum) are welcome and will be filed for six months; however, only candidates with experience relevant to current searches will be interviewed. Local firm established in 1991.

APPLEONE

155 108th N.E., #104
Bellevue WA 98004
(425) 451-7700, (800) 564-5644
Fax: (425) 451-9872
http://www.appleone.com
bmorris@mail.all-in-one.com
Contact: Bob Morris, regional manager

A California firm established in 1964, this agency has three locations in the Northwest. Most openings are in administrative support or clerical positions; there are also some opportunities in customer service. Placements are on a temporary, temp-to-hire and permanent basis. To apply: call or stop in with your resume. Allow two hours for an interview and testing.

APPLEONE

14180 N.E. Woodinville-Duvall Rd., #P3-46
Woodinville WA 98072
(425) 806-4695
Fax: (425) 402-9147
http://www.appleone.com

APPLEONE

321 S. Washington, #B-8
Kent WA 98032
(253) 854-4282
Fax: (253) 854-5817
http://www.appleone.com

Ashford Clark Personnel
4215 198th S.W., #102
Lynnwood WA 98036
(425) 774-9822; from the Eastside: (425) 827-6617; from Everett: (425) 353-8854
Fax: (425) 778-3924
acpinc@ix.netcom.com
Employment agency making placements on a temporary, temp-to-hire and permanent basis. Positions range from receptionist to manager, in such fields as high technology (for example, programmers), accounting, clerical, skilled labor and light industrial. Qualifications vary, but at a minimum you must be able to read and speak English. Administrative support jobs require that you type at least 40 words per minute and have expertise with Microsoft Word; experience with Excel is preferred. Fees may be employee- or employer-paid or split; ask when you register. To apply, telephone for an interview and test; allow for at least 90 minutes.

Automotive Personnel
1800 136th Pl. N.E., #4
Bellevue WA98005
(425) 643-4788
Contact: Mark Johnson
Established in the mid-1980s, this local firm specializes in the auto industry, recruiting staff for car dealerships. Positions range from lot attendants ($6-$7 an hour) to service cashiers, title clerks, technicians, finance and insurance specialists and salespeople. A general manager might be paid $100,000 or more, with the majority of the compensation in bonus form. Minimum qualifications: excellent driving record and clean police record. All fees are employer paid. To apply, call for an appointment.

Available Personnel, Inc.
801 S.W. 150th, #212
Burien WA 98166
(206) 433-8935
Fax: (206) 439-8902
acrossler@aol.com
This local employment agency handles mostly temporary assignments for clerical and light industrial jobs. Some temp-to-perm positions. Most work is in south King County. Established in 1990; all fees employer paid. To apply, call to schedule an interview and testing; allow 90 minutes to two hours.

B & M Unlimited
1218 Third Ave., #1518
Seattle WA 98101
(206) 223-1687
Fax: (206) 343-5555
bmunlim@aol.com
Contact: (Mr.) Lonnie Moore, president
Established in 1977, this local agency handles local government and private sector positions, in functions ranging from administrative support to accounting and finance (for example, CFO) to division management. All fees employer paid. If you submit a resume, it'll be retained for six months and reviewed regularly; you'll be contacted if the firm has a position that fits your background.

Bostwick Temporary Services
1109 First Ave., #406
Seattle WA 98101
(206) 340-1516
Fax: (206) 340-1522
bostwickinc@msn
Contact: (Mr.) Chris Bostwick, president
Legal positions, including contract attorneys (who, with experience and Washington state bar credentials, can make $30-$75 an hour), and administrative support positions are filled by this local agency. Support staff, who need experience in word processing, spreadsheet management programs and telephones, can make as much as $15 an hour. Positions may temporary or temp-to-hire. To apply, call for an appointment.

Business Careers
600 108th N.E., #246
Bellevue WA 98004
(425) 447-7411
Fax: (425) 447-5217
Contacts:
Jerry Moen, agency manager
Jerry Taylor, executive recruiter
Bellevue is the headquarters for this locally-owned agency, which handles executive search from this office. Each office fills positions separately, so you must apply at each. Executive recruiter Jerry Taylor works on a contingency basis, but job applicants may be asked to pay fees for lower level positions; ask when registering. Typical positions are in sales, including entry-level; management, including trainees; accounting; and technical, including entry-level engineers and tech support.

Business Careers
1001 Fourth Ave., #828
Seattle WA 98154
(206) 447-7474
Fax: (206) 447-7934
Contact: Randy Thompson, Seattle manager, Management Services

Business Careers
15 S. Grady Way, #333
Renton WA 98055
(425) 447-7433
Fax: (425) 255-3737
Contact: Laurie Robison, agency manager

Business Careers
1019 Pacific Ave., #1718
Tacoma WA 98402
(253) 383-1881; from Seattle: (206) 838-4045
Fax: (253) 383-2078
Contact: Jacquie Nolan, agency manager

Business Temps
1200 112th Ave. N.E., #P-100
Bellevue WA 98004
(425) 454-4300
Fax: (425) 454-3145
Contact: Julie Ostrowski, office manager
A local, woman-owned business founded in 1989. Focus: bookkeeping (to full-charge), administrative support and such general office functions as copy center staff. Places on a temporary and temp-to-hire basis. All fees employer paid. To apply, call for an appointment.

Career Clinic
9725 3rd Ave. N.E., #509
Seattle WA 98115
(206) 524-9831
Fax: (206) 524-4125
career@career.cnet.com
Established in 1967, this local agency fills temporary and permanent positions from support to senior level in four fields: high technology (for example, channel sales, network administrator, programmer), insurance (for example, claims manager or underwriter), construction (for example, estimator or project manager) and administrative support. Nearly all positions require at least three to five years of experience. Most fees are employer-paid; check when you register. No unsolicited applications or resumes are accepted; call for an appointment.

Careers Northwest
3405 188th St. S.W., #102
Lynnwood WA 98037
(425) 778-3100; from Everett: (425) 347-2941; from Marysville: (360) 653-5367
Fax: (425) 774-5795
Contacts:
Administrative support: Brenda Williams, agency manager
Marketing and high technology: Ed Beaulieu, department manager
An affiliate of Business Careers.

Career Temps
743 N. 35th St.
Seattle WA 98103
(206) 634-1752
Fax: (206) 634-1753
Contact: Sandy Edwards, vice president/manager
Woodinville to SeaTac is the market served by this local agency, which since 1992 has been providing clerical help on a temporary and temp-to-hire basis. You must be at least 18 to apply; allow 90 minutes for your interview and testing.

Catholic Archdiocese of Seattle

Office of the Superintendent of Schools
910 Marion St.
Seattle WA 98104
(206) 382-4856
Fax: (206) 654-4651
http://www.csdseattle.org
csd@connectinc.com
Distributes application packets for those interested in teaching in 64 Puget Sound
Catholic schools. Maintains applicants' files and publicizes teaching openings
with a weekly bulletin. Each year, handles 120-140 permanent openings, which are
filled after interviews at the individual schools. Also posts openings for substitute
teachers.

CDI Corp. West

4030 Lake Washington Blvd. N.E., #210
Kirkland WA 98033
(425) 739-7800
Fax: (425) 739-7818
cditek@aol.com
Hires technicians, assemblers, testers, quality control staff, machine operators and
shipping and receiving crews on a contract or temp-to-perm basis. Employer paid
fees.

Comforce/RHOTECH

4002 148th Ave. N.E.
Redmond WA 98073
(425) 883-2233
Fax: (425) 869-9898
http://www.comforce.com
jobs@redmond.rhotech.com
Formerly the locally-owned RHO Co., this firm was merged into a national agency
in 1997. Places people in positions ranging from entry-level clerical and light
industrial to professional and technical. Most opportunities are in the software
industry, in jobs such as tester or developer. Most upper-level positions require at
least two to four years experience. Assignment length: one week to ongoing. To be
added to Comforce's database, submit a cover letter identifying the positions you
seek and a scannable resume. All fees employer paid.

Cooper Personnel

1411 Fourth Ave., #1327
Seattle WA 98101
(206) 583-0722
Fax: (206) 223-4093
Contact: Bonnie Cooper
Established in 1988, this local firm has two specialties: administrative support, for
which candidates need expertise in word processing, database management,
spreadsheet management and Microsoft Power Point (either PC or Macintosh); and
international trade, especially for those who speak Japanese or other Asian
languages. The bilingual positions may be administrative, but there's an occa-

sional management opportunity. A related degree and one to three years experience are helpful. Makes placements from Tacoma to Everett and on the Eastside. To apply, call for an appointment.

CrediTemps
14900 Interurban Way, #217
Tukwila WA 98188
(206) 382-8477
Fax: (206) 248-1160
Contact: Eve Kiehm, manager
Focus: credit, including underwriting and collections. Provides entry-level to managerial staff on a temporary and temp-to-hire basis in King County. A branch of a Portland firm. All fees employer paid.

Deloitte & Touche Re:sources Connection LLC
700 Fifth Ave., #4500
Seattle WA 98104
(206) 233-7635
Fax: (206) 343-7809
http://www.dttus.com
jwonglee@dttus.com
Contact: Janie Lee, operations manager
Established in 1996, this subsidiary of a major accounting firm provides interim professionals and managers in accounting, finance and tax. For professional-level positions in audit or tax, projects often run from two weeks to six months. Hourly pay for such positions may start at $20. For recent graduates with limited experience, there's occasionally an opportunity to move from Re:sources to a regular Deloitte & Touche position. Some part-time opportunities. All fees employer paid. For information about senior-level interim placements, see *Contract Employment.*

Dental Connections
10116 36th Ave. Ct. S.W., #106
Lakewood WA 98499
(253) 588-2101
Fax: (253) 581-5572
http://www.dentalconnections.com
Contact: Donna Downing
Pierce, south King, Thurston, Kitsap and Grays Harbor counties are served by this temporary and permanent placement agency specializing in dentists, dental hygienists, dental assistants and dental receptionists. Dentists' jobs are usually one day, with pay ranging from $40 to $60 an hour. Both dentists and hygienists need Washington state licenses. Other positions require experience or completion of an accredited training course. All fees are employer paid. Established in 1982. To apply, call for a telephone screening.

Dental Employment Services
12827 S.E. 40th Pl., #200
Bellevue WA 98006
(425) 747-8095, (800) 303-8095
Fax: (425) 747-5843
Contact: Norma Dow
Established in 1981, this firm provides dental professionals and support staff on a permanent and temporary basis. Dentists are often hired for relief, as associates or to cover extra clinic hours. On a temporary basis, an experienced dentist might make $50 an hour; a recently graduated dental hygienist might make $32 an hour, while someone experienced with gum disease might make as much as $45. Applicants must have training; dentists and hygienists must be licensed. Temporary licenses may be available for hygienists licensed in other states. Serves practices from Olympia to Bellingham. To apply, call for an interview (allow an hour). All fees employer paid.

Dental Professionals
10032 15th S.W.
Seattle WA 98146
(206) 767-4851; from Bellevue: (425) 451-3391; from Everett: (425) 776-4583; from Tacoma: (253) 572-7004; toll-free (800) 762-4566
Contact: Shirley Templin, director
Focus: dental office staff, both support and professional, on a permanent and temporary basis. Dentists and hygienists must have Washington state licenses. For application information, call the office.

Drake Office Overload
520 Pike St., #1520
Seattle WA 98101
(206) 623-5552
Fax: (206) 623-7336
drakeint@myna.com
Contact: Elizabeth Eddy, director, Flexible Staffing
A branch of a Toronto firm. Established here in 1982 to provide clerical help on a temporary basis. Also provides light industrial and warehouse staff. Will relocate to another downtown Seattle location by 1998. Affiliated with Drake Personnel (see *Executive Search Firms: Locally Based*).

Employco Temporary Services
1511 Third Ave., #621
Seattle WA 98101
(206) 624-1700
Fax: (206) 624-7961
http://www.employcoinc.com
employco@sprynet.com
Contact: Sharee Olson
A woman-owned temporary and permanent staffing firm specializing in the law (from law clerks to attorneys), health care (for example, underwriters and medical claims processors) and bilingual administrative support and management (with most such positions requiring Japanese). An entry-level attorney might make $15

an hour, with an associate attracting $50,000 or more. Because the firm reports that good legal secretaries are difficult to find, someone with five to 10 years of Washington state litigation experience could earn $2,800-$3,500 per month. Employco reports a tough market for paralegals, however; without excellent experience, candidates are hard to place. Established in 1974, this local firm serves King County. Applicants should call for an interview and test; this will include Word for Windows and Excel.

Employers Overload
500 Union St., #435
Seattle WA 98101
(206) 583-0808
Focus: temporary office support. Applicants should arrange for an interview and test; allow two to three hours for the process. Qualified applicants will be asked for resumes. All fees employer paid.

Evergreen Staffing
1101 Fawcett, #350
Tacoma WA 98402
(253) 874-2900
Fax: (253) 383-0644
http://www.evergreenstaffing.com
info@evergreenstaffing.com
Contacts: Bill and Jan Rogers
This employment agency specializes in clerical and light industrial placements on a temporary and temp-to-hire basis. All fees are employer paid. To apply, call for an appointment at either office.

Evergreen Staffing
31620 23rd S.
Federal Way WA 98003
(253) 946-1400
Fax: (253) 946-1401
http://www.evergreenstaffing.com
bill@evergreenstaffing.com

Exceptional Temporary Escrow Services
1123 Maple Ave. S.W., #250
Renton WA 98055
(425) 226-9755
Fax: (425) 226-9804
Contact: Cathy Wiseman, vice president
If you have lots of experience in escrow, either in a professional or support position, consider contacting this local agency, which specializes in temporary and temp-to-hire positions from Olympia to Everett. Most positions pay $12-$18. All fees are employer paid. To apply, fax your resume; qualified candidates will be prescreened by telephone.

Express Personnel Services
1201 4th Ave. S., #101
Seattle WA 98134
(206) 343-5025
Fax: (206) 343-5321
http://www.monster.com/expresspersonnel
Contact: Kristina Ray Hribernick
One of 20 Express Personnel offices in Washington, most owned by different franchisees, this agency was established here in 1989 to specialize in temporary and permanent (40 per cent of the business) placement of technical (skilled labor and chemical lab assistants, but no software), clerical and light industrial staff. Serves clients from Tukwila to south of the Ship Canal (Magnolia and Queen Anne). All fees employer paid.

Express Personnel Services
4301 S. Pine St., #110
Tacoma WA 98409
(253) 475-6855
Fax: (253) 472-0721
http://www.monster.com/expresspersonnel
This franchise specializes in temporary and temp-to-hire placement of clerical and light industrial staff. All fees employer paid. Affiliated with the Puyallup office.

Express Personnel Services
315 39th Ave. S.W., #14
Puyallup WA 98373
(253) 840-8020
http://www.monster.com/expresspersonnel

Express Personnel Services
2726 Capital Mall Dr. S.W., #B4B
Olympia WA 98502
(360) 357-7195
Fax: (360) 357-6718
http://www.monster.com/expresspersonnel

Express Personnel Services
841 N. Central Ave., #100
Kent WA 98032
(253) 850-1344
Fax: (253) 850-1343
http://www.monster.com/expresspersonnel
Clerical: wandah@expresspersvc.com
Light industrial: christyee@expresspersvc.com
Contact: Wanda Halvorson
Affiliated with the Redmond franchise:

Express Personnel Services
15230 N.E. 24th, #F1-A
Redmond WA 98052
(425) 747-2424
Fax: (425) 747-3154
http://www.monster.com/expresspersonnel
Clerical: deanl@expresspersvc.com
Light industrial: dotc@expresspersvc.com

Express Personnel Services
4027 Hoyt Ave.
Everett WA 98201
(425) 339-8883
Fax: (425) 252-9817
http://www.monster.com/expresspersonnel
workjobs@aol.com
Contacts: Elizabeth Shinn and Bonnie McArthur
About 80 per cent of the placements in this office are temp-to-hire; the balance are contract or temporary (often seasonal). To apply, you can walk in or call for an appointment; interviews are conducted all day. Affiliated with the Monroe office.

Express Personnel Services
19501 Highway 2
Monroe WA 98272
(360) 805-1925
Fax: (360) 805-0932
http://www.monster.com/expresspersonnel
Contacts: Elizabeth Shinn and Bonnie McArthur

Express Personnel Services
4545 Auto Center Way, #B-1
Bremerton WA 98312
(360) 479-4756
Fax: (360) 479-4759
http://www.monster.com/expresspersonnel
Contacts: Wayne and Phylis Sargent

Express Personnel Services
19105 36th Ave. W., Bldg. 2, #105
Lynnwood WA 98036
(425) 775-4903
Fax: (425) 778-3090
http://www.monster.com/expresspersonnel
expersvc@gte.net
Contact: Donna Knutsen

Favorite Nurses
2150 N. 107th St., #345
Seattle WA 98133
(206) 440-1180
Fax: (206) 440-1250
http://www.favoritenurses.com
A branch of a Kansas firm; in Seattle since the early 1980s. Places nursing personnel, from RNs to home health aides, usually on one-day assignments in hospitals and nursing homes. Applicants must have at least one year of recent experience in the function in which they wish to work and appropriate licenses and certification. You can apply using the online application form or visit the office; allow at least two hours for the interview and tests.

Firstaff
401 Parkplace, #301
Kirkland WA 98033
(425) 822-0300; from Seattle: (206) 622-7488
Jobline: (425) 517-7770
Fax: (425) 827-7911
Contact: Deirdre Staudt, president
Specialty: clerical and accounting positions (to accounting manager), both temporary and permanent. Positions require relevant experience and you'll need a resume when you apply. Allow two hours for your interview and tests. All fees employer paid.

Garden Variety Personnel
320 108th N.E., #600
Bellevue WA 98004
(425) 454-3181
If you have at least a year of full-time experience in a floral, landscaping or nursery business, consider this agency, which provides temporary and permanent staff in that industry. Formal education in the field is helpful, too. Fees are employer paid. Affiliated with ReproTemps.

General Employment Service Inc.
600 University St., #2525
Seattle WA 98101
(206) 467-1255
Fax: (206) 467-1255
http://www.bradson.com
Established locally in 1945; now a subsidiary of a Canadian firm. Offers temporary, temp-to-hire, contract and permanent placements in such areas as administrative support, accounting, law, customer service, insurance, human resources, information technology and light industrial. Assignments range from a few hours to a year. Prefers candidates who have good computer skills and keyboard at least 40 words per minute. Also seeks experience with a multi-line phone system, excellent grammar and good public relations skills. Bring a resume and list of your skills when you come to interview. All fees employer paid.

Gilmore Temporary Personnel
2722 Colby Ave., #414
Everett WA 98201
(425) 252-1195
Fax: (425) 259-7901
Established in the early 1970s. Handles temporary and temp-to-hire clerical positions. Prefers that candidates have two to three years experience, proficiency with Microsoft Office 97 and can keyboard at least 45-60 words per minute. All fees employer paid.

Globe Temporaries
2001 Sixth Ave., #306
Seattle WA 98121
(206) 443-4314
Fax: (206) 448-8418
Contacts:
Linda Schaufele, manager
Barbara Gorrell, owner
Founded in 1990, this local firm provides administrative support staff (from clerks to administrative assistants) on a temporary and temp-to-hire basis. Pay: $8-$15 an hour. To apply, call for an appointment (allow 60 to 90 minutes). You'll need a resume plus three professional references (for example, previous supervisors) and two personal references (co-workers, for example).

Goto & Company
7981 168th Ave. N.E., #27
Redmond WA 98052
(425) 869-8092
Fax: (425) 881-9500
hiroshigoto@msn.com
Contact: Hiroshi Goto
Nearly all the clients for this local search firm are Japanese firms seeking staff for Northwest offices. Some positions are entry-level; others are supervisory or at the vice president level. Some candidates must be bilingual. All fees are employer paid. Resumes may be submitted by fax, mail or e-mail.

Guidance Services Inc.
1010 S. 336th, #122
Federal Way WA 98003
(253) 838-2401
(253) 925-8610
A division of a New York firm. Offers temporary and permanent placements of clerical staff and medical office support staff. Call for an appointment.

Hallmark Placements
1904 Third Ave., #819
Seattle WA 98101
(206) 587-5360
Fax: (206) 587-5319
Contact: Dolores Gohndrone, manager
Focus: temporary and permanent placements in engineering for the software

industry (often requiring a degree in electrical engineering or computer science), food service (including bartenders, chefs and management) and administration (from clerks to accounting managers). Most positions pay $60,000 or less. Most engineering jobs require five to 10 years experience, most sales jobs three to five years similar experience and the most senior level accounting positions require at least five years experience. At the lower level, half of the fees are paid by the job-seeker; check when you apply. To apply, call for an appointment. Lower level positions require skills testing. Locally owned; founded in 1981.

Help Staffing Services
4700 42nd Ave. S.W., #500
Seattle WA 98116
(206) 938-5054
Fax: (206) 938-0872
Places clerical and light industrial workers in temporary and temp-to-hire positions. To apply, call for an appointment; allow two hours for your interview and test. All fees employer paid.

Hospitality Services Inc.
6625 S. 190th, #B-108
Kent WA 98032
(425) 251-1901
Fax: (425) 251-1903
Contact: Marvin Miller, president
Looking for a job with a restaurant, hotel, hospital, country club or with a caterer? This local firm makes temporary and permanent placements in positions ranging from busser to CEO, from Olympia to Bellingham. Most opportunities are in hotel front desk and sales positions and in restaurant management. At a minimum, candidates should have a stable work history (not five employers in five years, warns Marvin Miller), good customer service skills and a pleasant appearance. To apply, call for an interview. Also shares a North End office with:

Human Resources Inc.
10564 5th Ave. N.E., #204
Seattle WA 98125
(206) 368-9039
Fax: (206) 368-9243

Human Resources Inc.
9725 S.E. 36th, #100
Mercer Island WA 98040
(206) 236-8094
Fax: (206) 236-7658
hri@cyberspace.com
Contact: Sheri Hervey, vice president
Specializes in computer-proficient administrative and accounting positions (from entry-level $7 an hour jobs) to managerial level accounting and human resources positions (controllers, CFOs and HR managers earning as much as $50,000). Temporary, temp-to-perm and permanent placements in Seattle and Bellevue, with occasional opportunities in Kent, Preston and Edmonds. Entry and mid-level jobs require proficiency with Microsoft Office, good customer service skills, experi-

ence with multi-line phone systems, a stable work history and a "can do" attitude. If you're willing to commute, you'll be easier to place. To apply, fax or mail in a resume; when you're scheduled for an interview, allow two hours. All fees employer paid. Although affiliated with the same parent, this office and each of the following may have different owners.

Human Resources Inc.
451 S.W. 10th, #112
Renton WA 98055
(425) 228-2289
Fax: (425) 228-3513
http://www.otsego.net/hri
nfkj44a@prodigy.com
Contact: Stacy Molzan
Focus: sales management, technical and administrative jobs. Temporary, temp-to-hire and permanent. To apply, submit a resume and then call for an interview. All fees employer paid. Owned by same couple who owns the Tacoma agency:

Human Resources Inc.
2115 S. 56th St., #403
Tacoma WA 98409
(253) 471-2611
Fax: (253) 474-0109

Human Resources Inc.
2703 Capitol Mall Dr., #3-A
Olympia WA 98502
(360) 753-6720
Fax: (360) 753-1592
Temporary, temp-to-hire and permanent placement of administrative support.

Human Resources Inc.
10564 5th Ave. N.E., #204
Seattle WA 98125
(206) 368-9039
Fax: (206) 368-9243
humanra@aol.com
Contact: E. Pete Stiles
Focus: administrative support to mid-management positions on a temporary, temp-to-perm and permanent basis. Candidates must be computer-literate; most jobs require proficiency with Microsoft and Lotus software. You must be able to keyboard at least 35 words a minute; grammar, spelling and math skills will be tested. To apply, call for an appointment; allow at least 90 minutes. All fees employer paid. Also owns:

Human Resources Inc.
2 Auburn Way N., #102
Auburn WA 98002
(253) 804-3477
Fax: (253) 804-3476
humanra@aol.com

Insurance Overload Systems
19515 North Creek Parkway, #314
Bothell WA 98011
(425) 806-3971
Fax: (425) 806-3972
Contact: (Ms.) Kelly Lynch, branch manager
Headquartered in Dallas with an office here since 1994. Specialty: the insurance industry (life, health, property casualty, for brokerage firms, agencies and corporate worker's compensation programs), in positions ranging from clerks to manager. Places on a temporary (25 per cent of the business) and temp-to-perm basis. Candidates should have industry experience—a year for entry-level positions, at least three to five years for higher level jobs. To apply, call for a telephone interview; qualified candidates will be asked to fax in their resumes and schedule in-person interviews.

Insurance Staffing Inc.
2200 Sixth Ave., #407
Seattle WA 98121
(206) 728-1404
Fax: (206) 728-1406
insstaff@juno.com
Contacts: Eileen Lewis and Patricia Orozco-Daly
Established in 1995, this local firm files insurance industry positions from file clerks to department managers. Most positions pay less than $50,000. An entry-level position requires a career orientation, high energy level, good customer service skills and proficiency with Microsoft Office and other basic office software. You should be able to keyboard 50 words per minute. A degree is important, but not mandatory for lower-level jobs. To apply, call for an interview; allow at least 90 minutes for your screening and tests.

Interacc
P.O. Box 64367
University Place WA 98464
(253) 565-2060; from Seattle: (206) 838-1300
Fax: (253) 565-1998
Contact: Rick Wells, manager
A local firm founded in 1977. Focus: clerical and accounting positions (to office manager and accountant) in Pierce and south King counties. To apply, call for an appointment.

Interim Court Reporting
500 Union St., #926
Seattle WA 98101
(206) 624-3377
Fax: (206) 623-7228
http://www.interim.com
One of 1,000 Interim offices across the U.S., all branches of the Fort Lauderdale-headquartered firm. This office places court reporters. All fees employer paid. Affiliated with the following Interim agencies:

Interim HealthCare
10700 Meridian Ave. N., #107
Seattle WA 98133
(206) 440-9498
Fax: (206) 440-8611
http://www.interim.com
Places nurses, LPNs, CNAs, RNAs and homemaker-companions, usually on a temporary basis, in hospitals, nursing homes, clinics, adult family homes and retirement homes. Applicants can also register at:

Interim HealthCare
4301 S. Pine St., #456
Tacoma WA 98409
(253) 473-4500
Fax: (253) 475-3190

Interim Personnel
557 Roy St., #135
Seattle WA 98109
(206) 282-9881
Fax: (206) 282-7256
http://www.interim.com
Contact: Kris Brunlov, clerical manager
Specialties: office support (to office administrator and executive assistant) and light industrial (assembly to fork-lift operator, in positions paying $6-$10 an hour). Temporary and permanent placements. You'll be easiest to place in an office position if you are proficient with Microsoft Office, can keyboard 50 words per minute, have at least two years office experience and a professional appearance, if you're articulate and if you're flexible about duties and shifts.

Interim Personnel
777 108th Ave. N.E., #1200
Bellevue WA 98004
(425) 462-7004
Fax: (425) 462-0752
http://www.interim.com
jmiller@ji.com

Interim Personnel
1500 S. 336th St., #12
Federal Way WA 98003
(253) 874-8705
Fax: (253) 874-8495
http://www.interim.com
Focus: clerical and light industrial. Has two satellite offices for recruiting:

Interim Personnel
6100 Southcenter Blvd., #A-235
Tukwila WA 98188
(206) 439-8668
Fax: (206) 439-8788
http://www.interim.com

Interim Personnel
727 Commerce St., #200
Tacoma WA 98402
(253) 952-3112
http://www.interim.com

Jobs Unlimited
870 S.W. 136th St.
Seattle WA 98166
(206) 243-8225
Fax: (206) 244-2767
A local firm established in 1978 to make permanent placements of such trades-people as carpenters, machinists and truck drivers. You can call for an appointment or walk in between 8 a.m. and 4:30 p.m.; come in prepared to be sent out on an interview. You can register at either the Seattle or Tacoma office and work from both:

Jobs Unlimited
5310 12th St. E., #A
Fife WA 98424
(253) 922-0575
Fax: (253) 870-0106

Kelly Services
601 Union St., #3604
Seattle WA 98104
General inquiries: (206) 382-7171; for appointments: (800) 505-6200
Fax: (206) 382-9679
http://www.kellyservices.com
kelrec@ix.netcom.com
One of 10 Puget Sound offices, this agency ofers temporary, temp-to-perm and permanent placement in such fields as office support (the highest positions pay $18 per hour), light industrial, customer service, electronics (including tech support and board stuffers), and technical (which incudes positions as high as accounting manager). You can register at any of Kelly's 900 offices across the U.S. and be considered for assignments here. All fees are employer paid. When interviewing, candidates need two references (preferably business) and experience (six or 12 months minimum for office support and two or three years for higher-level positions). You also need to be committed to a job, adaptable and flexible (recruiters remind that you may be working somewhere different every week), able to think on your feet, take initiative and communicate well, both with your employers and with the Kelly staff. To be placed immediately, you'll need proficiency with Microsoft Office; Internet skills are important and so is experi-

ence with graphics software and Microsoft Project. When you come in for an interview and test, allow two to four hours.

Kelly Services
10900 N.E. 4th, #250
Bellevue WA 98004
(425) 454-7230
Fax: (425) 454-6090

Kelly Services
16040 Christensen Rd., #205
Seattle WA 98188
(800) 505-6200
Fax, administrative applicants: (206) 243-7674
Fax, technical applicants: (206) 243-7534
Includes Kelly Aerospace Division, which supplies administrative personnel to aircraft manufacturers.

Kelly Services
1010 S.E. Everett Mall Way, #203
Everett WA 98208
Administrative applicants: (425) 347-9333
Aerospace applicants: (800) 505-6200
Fax, administrative applicants: (425) 348-7353
Fax, aerospace applicants: (425) 347-1569
Includes Kelly Aerospace Division, which supplies administrative personnel to aircraft manufacturers.

Kelly Services
555 S. Renton Village Pl., #225
Renton WA 98055
(425) 226-2205
Fax: (425) 226-3268

Kelly Services
2702 S. 42nd, #208
Tacoma WA 98409
(253) 471-0415
Fax: (253) 473-4454

Kelly Services
4405 7th Ave., #303
Olympia WA 98503
(360) 493-0160
Fax: (360) 491-3150

King County Medical Society Employment Agency
200 Broadway
Seattle WA 98122
(206) 621-9470
Fax: (206) 292-9780

Interviews and refers job-seekers to openings in medical offices and clinics. Most are technical (for example, certified medical assistant) or administrative (medical receptionist or insurance biller); a few openings for such professionals as RNs. Applicants can ask to be referred only to fee-paid opportunities.

Labor Express
see Allied Forces/Labor Express

Labor Ready
7617 Aurora Ave. N.
Seattle WA 98103
(206) 781-8895
Interested in daily pay for daily work? This labor hall handles construction clean-up, janitorial and similar work paying $6 an hour. It's better to apply a day in advance of when you want to work. To apply, you'll need valid state picture identification and a Social Security card or other proof of legal authority to work in the U.S. All applicants must pass a short written safety quiz. Opens at 5 a.m.; work is assigned on a first come, first assigned basis. Additional branches in Bothell, Everett, Kent, Renton and Tacoma.

LabTemps
P.O. Box 40285
Bellevue WA 98015
(425) 637-9990
Fax: (425) 688-0636
If you've seen a LabTemps ad for a position for which you're qualified, you can call and then follow up with a resume. Most positions are for phlebotomists (usually requires one or two years experience) or medical or environmental technicians. Some positions require a B.S., others a M.S. Pay: $7-$25 per hour. Clients from Federal Way to Everett. Temporary and permanent positions. A local firm established in 1991; all fees employer paid. Affiliated with Nu West.

Lakeside Personnel
1818 Westlake Ave. N., #126
Seattle WA 98109
(206) 284-6066
Fax: (206) 282-8289
Contacts:
Sig Bergquist, president
Ed M. Lee, retail recruitment specialist
Specialty: retail—from trainee to mid-management, in positions paying $22,000-$45,000. Most jobs are at the store-level along the Interstate 5 corridor. Most require retail experience; a degree is helpful. Resumes accepted by mail and fax.

Law Dawgs
1201 Third Ave., #2810
Seattle WA 98101
(206) 224-8244
Fax: (206) 224-8291
http://www.jetcity.com/~lawdawgs.html
lawdawgs@jetcity.com
Contact: Ewen Cameron, president
Places legal professionals, including paralegals and contract attorneys, on a
temporary, temp-to-hire and permanent basis in law firms and corporations. Some
attorneys work as long as eight months on contract; some are hired after working
on contract. A local firm established in 1995. To apply, call for more information;
applicants are screened prior to being interviewed. All fees employer paid.

Legal Northwest
520 Pike St., #2605
Seattle WA 98101
(206) 448-0200
Fax: (206) 448-0200
http://www.ntss.com
Provides legal support on a temporary basis. Positions include document clerks,
messengers, word processors and legal secretaries.

Legal Northwest
600 108th Ave. N.E., #239
Bellevue WA 98004
(425) 453-2310
Fax: (425) 451-9285
http://www.ntss.com
Provides legal support on a temporary basis.

Legal Northwest
9930 Evergreen Way, Bldg. C-106
Everett WA 98206
(425) 774-3511
Fax: (425) 670-2652
http://www.ntss.com
Provides legal support on a temporary basis.

Legal Secretarial Staffing
P.O. Box 31493
Seattle WA 98103
(206) 633-3324
Fax: (206) 633-5411
Contact: Deana Richardson
Provides legal support (from messengers and document clerks to paralegals and
administrators) to law firms and corporations on a temporary, temp-to-hire and
permanent basis. No placements of attorneys or law firm accountants. Candidates
must be Windows-proficient. A paralegal with five years experience and Washington state litigation experience might make $36,000-$40,000, but openings are rare.

By contract, at press time legal secretaries were difficult to find; someone with three to five years experience could expect to make about $36,000 in 1998. To apply, submit a resume. When interviewed, you'll need two or three references covering the last three to five years and proof of legal authority to work in the U.S. All fees employer paid.

LegalStaff
8625 Evergreen Way, #203
Everett WA 98208
(425) 355-7223; from Seattle: (206) 745-5141; toll-free: (800) 755-7638
Fax: (425) 353-1612
http://www.terrasvc.com
resume@terrasvc.com
Affiliated with Terra Personnel Group. Provides legal support on a temporary basis, in positions ranging from receptionist to legal secretary and paralegal. All fees employer paid.

Manpower Inc.
1420 Fifth Ave., #1750
Seattle WA 98101
(206) 583-0880
Jobline: (206) 447-JOBS
Fax: (206) 622-3629
http://www.manpower.com
Contact: Donna Braungardt, manager
Headquartered in Milwaukee, Manpower has owned offices in the Puget Sound area for decades. Between Olympia and Bellingham, there are 11 plus client-satellites. This is the largest local office. You should register with the office that serves your geographic area unless you're applying for technical jobs, which are all placed from Kirkland regardless of where you register. Most offices focus on administrative support (or "office automation"), telemarketing and customer service (for example, outbound sales, help desk or catalog sales jobs) and light industrial. Placements may be temporary or temp-to-perm. A light industrial position might involve shipping and receiving or order picking, with pay at $7-$9 an hour. The office automation jobs which often lead to permanent positions require a high level of skill with Microsoft Office; pay is $8.50-$16. Soft-sell outbound calling may pay $8-$14 plus bonus. Candidates must be 18 or older, have legal authority to work in the U.S. and have a stable work history. Previous employers will be contacted and you'll be tested on your skills. Allow 90 minutes to two hours for your first interview and tests. All fees employer paid.

Manpower Inc.
11400 S.E. 8th, #330
Bellevue WA 98004
(425) 451-1708
Fax: (425) 451-1246
Contact: Betsy Pidgeon, manager

Manpower Inc.
3400 188th Ave. S.W., #222
Lynnwood WA 98037
(425) 771-1708
Fax: (425) 775-9987
http://www.manpower.com
Contact: Gerald Perez, manager

Manpower Inc.
2731 Wetmore Ave., #204
Everett WA 98201
(425) 252-4740
Fax: (425) 252-4772
Contact: Mary Howell, manager

Manpower Inc.
10049 Kitsap Mall Blvd., #108
Silverdale WA 98383
(360) 698-2592
Fax: (360) 698-7369
Contact: Linda Patterson, manager

Manpower Inc.
12720 Gateway Dr., #103
Tukwila WA 98168
(206) 241-9005
Fax: (206) 241-6217
Contact: Amanda Hostetler, manager

Manpower Inc.
500 S. 336th St., #101
Federal Way WA 98003
(253) 838-1228
Fax: (253) 952-6935
Contact: Barbara Tramelli, manager

Manpower Inc.
4002 Tacoma Mall Blvd., #103A
Tacoma WA 98409
(253) 473-5023
Fax: (253) 473-2808
Contact: Andrea Pollard, manager

Manpower Inc.
905 24th Way S.W., #A-2
Olympia WA 98502
(360) 357-5373
Fax: (360) 357-9993

Manpower Technical Division

911 5th Ave., #102
Kirkland WA 98033
(425) 889-9745
Fax: (425) 822-8708
http://www.manpower.com
Contact: Carla Scharb, manager
The most common openings are for programmers (SQL, UNIX, C++), network specialists, and help desk support staff, who make $15-$25. Temporary, temp-to-perm and permanent. All fees employer paid.

MedStaff

2150 N. 107th
Seattle WA 98133
(206) 361-8419
Fax: (206) 361-8113
http://www.medstaff-inc.com
Contact: Lynn Burns, manager
Specialty: temporary and permanent staff for medical and dental clinics, including clinic managers, business managers and dental hygienists. A medical receptionist with some experience can expect to make at least $10 an hour, a medical assistant $11 an hour and up and billers and bookkeepers, at least $12 an hour. Besides experience, candidates need a good work enthic, professional appearance and good communication skills. Occasional openings for new graduates from accredited schools (Lynn Burns will check on your externs prior to placement). A local firm established in 1991; all fees employer paid.

MedTemps

P.O. Box 40374
Bellevue WA 98015
(425) 688-1800
Fax: (425) 688-0636
Affiliated with Nu West. Provides temporary and permanent support and professional staff (from receptionists to nurses) for private medical practices and hospitals. All fees employer paid.

Millennium Staffing

601 Union St., #1625
Seattle WA 98101
(206) 464-4055
Fax: (206) 464-4147
millennium@seanet.com
Contact: Steve Curran, staffing consultant
Part of a national launched in 1997; affiliated with Accountants On Call. Provides project and permanent placement of "administrative and creative services professionals" for web-site and desktop publishing creation and higher-level administrative support. Candidates need to be able to communicate well and have strong software and creative skills. How to approach: send in your resume first; the most qualified candidates will be interviewed.

Millionair Club Charity Employment Program
2515 Western Ave.
Seattle WA 98121
(206) 728-5627
Fax: (206) 443-1978
A nonprofit labor hall that dispatches temporary workers. Requirements: no felony convictions, a Social Security card, valid state picture identification and your own transportation (for example, bus fare). Men should apply between 6:30 a.m. and 2:30 p.m.; three new applicants are processed each day. To be assigned to work, men start lining up at 5 a.m. the days they seek work. Women can apply between 6 a.m. and 2 p.m.; all applicants will be processed each day. Pay: $7 an hour. All jobs are for at least four hours. No fees to job-seekers or employers.

Mini-Systems Associates
14535 Bel-Red Rd., #200
Bellevue WA 98007
(425) 644-9500
Fax: (425) 644-0200
http://www.mini-systems.com/msa
resumes@wa.mini-systems.com
A branch of a California firm. Provides contract (two weeks to several months) and permanent placements in high technology, including software developers, engineers and testers, technical writers and telecommunications splicers, technicians and installers. For software positions, there's little entry-level work. Pay may be $20-40 an hour.

Molly Brown Temps, Inc.
12627 N.E. 20th, #2
Bellevue WA 98005
(425) 883-2427
Fax: (425) 867-1587
This local firm, founded in 1984, is headquartered here and there's a satellite office in Seattle. Specialty: administrative support on a temporary, temp-to-hire and permanent basis. Candidates are easier to place if they have office experience and keyboarding skills. To apply, call for an appointment; allow 90 minutes for your interview and tests.

Molly Brown Temps, Inc.
520 Pike St., #1330
Seattle WA 98101
(206) 628-0598
Fax: (206) 628-0584
mollyb@nwlink.com

Morgen Design Inc.
150 Andover Park W.
Seattle WA 98188
(206) 433-7863
Fax: (206) 433-8809
http://www.w-link.net/~morgen
morgen@w-link.net
Contacts:
Elaine Tsang, employment specialist, engineering
Sylvia Washington, employment specialist, laborers
Headquartered in Salt Lake City, this firm has two divisions: an in-house engineering office, for which it hires permanent and contract employees, and the placement agency. Engineering jobs require experience and a degree in electrical, aeronautical or mechanical engineering. Also places some laborers and clerical staff. Employer paid fees.

Nelson, Coulson & Associates
14450 N.E. 29th Pl., #115
Bellevue WA 98007
(425) 883-6612
Fax: (425) 883-6916
http://www.ncainc.com
denise@ncainc.com
Contact: Denise Buettgenbach, manager
A branch of a Denver firm. Focus: high technology, including aerospace engineers, electronic technicians, administrative assistants and customer service staff. Places on a temporary (two or three months or longer), contract (six months to several years) and permanent basis. Typical pay: an aerospace engineer with five to 10 years experience and a degree might make $35 an hour on contract. Works on a contingency basis.

Norrell Services
14670 N.E. 8th, #200
Bellevue WA 98007
(425) 643-0133
Fax: (425) 643-7919
A national firm with two local offices. Specialty: administrative and accounting support positions on a temporary and temp-to-hire basis. Most positions require proficiency with Microsoft Office, at least two years experience and a professional demeanor and appearance. (Some Norrell clients have strict dress codes, recruiters note.) Pay: $6.50 an hour for entry-level jobs to $14 or more for administrative assistant positions. Employer paid fees.

Norrell Services
900 Fourth Ave., #1440
Seattle WA 98164
(206) 340-9074
Fax: (206) 233-0389

Northwest Demo Service
12835 Bellevue-Redmond Rd.
Bellevue WA 98005
(425) 455-5270
Contact: Anita Jerome
Established in 1970, this local firm provides temporary workers to conduct in-store demonstrations and in-store couponing in western Washington grocery chains. You might work one to 10 days a month, usually Friday through Sunday, on six to eight-hour shifts. Requires high school graduation, reliable transportation, the ability to stand several hours and an outgoing personality.

Northwest Temporary & Staffing Services
520 Pike St., #2605
Seattle WA 98101
(206) 448-0200
Fax: (206) 441-6344
http://www.ntss.com
Founded in 1985 in Portland, this firm includes a clerical, accounting support and light industrial operation under this name as well as speciality placement divisions operatings under the names Accountants Northwest, Legal Northwest and Resource Technology Group. This clerical/light industrial operation has four Puget Sound offices. All fees employer paid.

Northwest Temporary & Staffing Services
600 10th Ave. N.E., #239
Bellevue WA 98004
(425) 453-2310
Fax: (425) 451-9285
http://www.ntss.com

Northwest Temporary & Staffing Services
9930 Evergreen Way, Bldg. C-106
Everett WA 98206
(425) 774-3511
Fax: (425) 670-2652
http://www.ntss.com

Northwest Temporary & Staffing Services
6625 S. 190th St., #B-108
Kent WA 98032
(425) 251-6651
Fax: (425) 251-6839
http://www.ntss.com

Nu West
1200 112th Ave. N.E., #C-110
Bellevue WA 98004
(425) 637-9500
Fax: (425) 637-9793
A local company established in 1991. Four divisions: Nu West, providing account-

ing, administrative and customer service staff; LabTemps; MedTemps and WesTech. Opportunities here are usually temporary or temp-to-hire. Accounting positions include full-charge bookkeepers and occasionally a controller job; administrative positions may be as senior as executive assistants (a position paying in the mid to high 30s for someone with project management experience, proficiency with Microsoft Office and keyboarding skills of at least 50 words per minute).

O.R.M./MORE Staffing
5700 6th Ave. S., #220
Seattle WA 98108
(206) 763-3771
Fax: (206) 763-3844
Contacts: Steve Haemmerlein and Jim Crabbe, dispatchers
A local firm established in the mid-90s to provide temporary workers for stevedoring, marine crane, fork lift operator and other marine jobs as well as moving and cold storage warehouse positions. Occasional temp-to-hire positions. Requires applicable experience, skill and good references. Pays $8-$12 an hour. All fees employer paid.

Office Team
601 Union St., #4300
Seattle WA 98101
(206) 749-9060
Fax: (206) 749-9373
http://www.officeteam.com
seattle@officeteam.com
Provides administrative support to the executive secretary level on a temporary and temp-to-hire basis. An excellent candidate proficient in Windows and Microsoft Office, capable of complex travel arrangements and experienced in supporting one or two top executives, can earn as much as $45,000-$50,000. To apply, call for a telephone screening and appointment, which will include testing. Allow two hours. Dress as you would for a job interview. All fees employer paid. Other local offices:

Office Team
2505 S. 320th St., #120
Federal Way WA 98003
(253) 946-0333
Fax: (253) 946-2095
http://www.officeteam.com
federalway@officeteam.com

Office Team
10900 N.E. 4th St., #1650
Bellevue WA 98004
(425) 455-3860
Fax: (425) 455-1989
http://www.officeteam.com
bellevue@officeteam.com

Office Team
3400 188th S.W., #165
Lynnwood WA 98037
(425) 712-7259
Fax: (425) 712-7165
http://www.officeteam.com

Olsten Staffing Services
601 Union St., #732
Seattle WA 98101
(206) 464-1616, (800) WORK-NOW
Fax: (206) 464-1711
http://www.worknow.com
Headquartered in New York, Olsten has several branches in the Puget Sound area
with specialties including product assembly and distribution, general clerical,
office automation (typically requiring proficiency with Microsoft Office and
keyboarding at 40 words per minute), technical (from sautering PC boards to
skilled positions), accounting (most commonly, bookkeepers and credit analysts)
and legal support (including legal secretaries and paralegals). All fees are employer paid.

Olsten Staffing Services
1000 S.E. Everett Mall Way, #205
Everett WA 98208
(425) 710-9917, (800) WORK-NOW
Fax: (425) 710-9021
http://www.worknow.com

Olsten Staffing Services
4020 Lake Washington Blvd., #301
Kirkland WA 98033
(425) 889-4544, (800) WORK-NOW
Fax: (425) 889-4543
http://www.worknow.com

Olsten Staffing Services
19115 West Valley Highway, #H-110
Kent WA 98032
(425) 656-4199, (800) WORK-NOW
Fax: (425) 656-4397
http://www.worknow.com

Pac Personnel Inc.
17965 N.E. 65th
Redmond WA 98052
(425) 556-1775
Fax: (425) 556-1778
http://www.pac.com
stevem@pac.com
Contact: Steve Mullen, account administrator
Serves the Eastside with staff for technical jobs (assembly to programming) paying

$6.50 to $20 an hour as well as clerical and light industrial. Temporary, temp-to-hire and permanent placements. To apply, call for an appointment or submit your resume via fax or e-mail. Allow at least an hour for an interview and testing. Some walk-in interviews conducted; call for information. A local firm established in 1992.

Pace Staffing Network
720 Third Ave., #2220
Seattle WA 98104
(206) 623-1050
Fax: (206) 467-8379
Provides staff in administrative support, health care and customer service.

Parker Services
1501 Fourth Ave., #450
Seattle WA 98101
(206) 447-9447
Jobline: (206) 447-1917, Ext. 123
Fax: (206) 223-8227
parkersea@pnw.com
A local company with three divisions: Resource Management Services, which provides professional and managerial staff; Human Resource Partnering, which audits and establishes HR departments on a consulting basis; and Parker Services, which provides trade association/convention support (including registration assistance and badge-making), administrative (including customer service and call center staff and executive assistants), medical support (nonclinical office positions) and legal support (from clerks to paralegals) on a temporary and permanent basis. Candidates are more easily placed when they have at least a year's experience.

Parker Services
6720 Ft. Dent Way, #175
Tukwila WA 98188
(206) 901-1927
Fax: (206) 901-1941
mkru@msn.com

Parker Services
400 112th N.E., #340
Bellevue WA 98004
(425) 462-8050
Fax: (425) 637-5177
parkerblvu@pnw.com

Parker Services
1501 Market St., #360
Tacoma WA 98402
(253) 272-0979, (800) 488-8298
Fax: (253) 383-0611
parkertac@pnw.com

Parsons Personnel
10900 N.E. 4th, #2243
Bellevue WA 98004
(425) 451-3920
Fax (after office hours): (425) 451-7486
kparsons@iswnet.com
Contact: Karen Parsons
Specializes in administrative support (to executive assistant and secretary to the CEO), sales and accounting (to controller with CPA). A typical executive assistant position might require excellent computer skills, including proficiency with Microsoft Office, good interpersonal skills and five to 10 years experience. A degree in business and fluency in a foreign language makes you easier to place. Salary range: $25,000-$45,000. Most placements are permanent; some are long-term temporary and temp-to-hire. To apply, call first and then submit a resume and cover letter. A telephone screening may follow a review of your resume. Mailed resumes should be scannable. E-mailed resumes should be formatted using Windows 95 and sent as an attachment to the cover letter. The letter should indicate either salary history or expectations, the kind of position sought and three to six reasons why you should be hired. All fees employer paid.

Personnel Management Systems, Inc. (PMSI)
1750 112th Ave. N.E., #E-175
Bellevue WA 98004
(425) 451-1441
Fax: (425) 451-3654
http://www.hrpmsi.com
heatherc@pmsi.wa.com
Founded in the 1980s, this off-site human resources firm provides HR services (including recruiting) for smaller employers (usually 50-200 employees) along the I-5 corridor. All fees employer paid. For most positions (excluding technical), PMSI advertises the opening, receives the resumes, screens candidates (by telephone or initial interview) and recommends three to six candidates for the employer's own interviewing process. For such technical positions as software engineering, employers do all screening. Job-seekers can review open positions in the lobby of the Bellevue headquarters or can check the web site. Other offices in Portland and Tacoma, with an Everett office scheduled to open in 1998.

Personnel Management Systems, Inc. (PMSI)
1530 S. Union St., #12
Tacoma WA 98405
(253) 759-9984
Fax: (253) 759-8189
http://www.hrpmsi.com
krise@pmsi.wa.com

Pharmacy Relief Consultants of Washington
7130 Wright S.W.
Seattle WA 98136
(206) 933-6936
Contact: Gloria Malloy, office manager

Established in 1991, this local firm handles temporary (one day to several weeks) placements of pharmacists. Candidates must be licensed in Washington state; experience is preferred.

Pierce County Medical Society Medical Placement Service
223 Tacoma Ave. S.
Tacoma WA 98402
(253) 572-3709
Fax: (253) 572-2470
Places medical receptionists, bookkeepers, LPNs and RNs in private medical practices. An applicant should have at least six months experience in his or her function or be a recent graduate of an appropriate program. To register, you'll need a resume and references, identification and copies of your certication or diploma. No fee for temporary placements. For permanent placements, fees may be paid by applicant or employer.

Pro Staff
999 Third Ave., #1005
Seattle WA 98104
(206) 624-4300
Fax: (206) 624-4390
http://www.prostaff.com
karen_hemmett@prostaff.com
elizabeth_radford@prostaff.com
Contacts:
Karen Hemmett, staffing manager
Beth Radford, staffing supervisor
Headquartered in Minnesota with two offices in this area. You can register at either. Specialty: administrative support (to administrative and executive assistants and legal secretaries), accounting (to full-charge bookkeepers and accounting managers) and technical support (for example, help desk crews). Prefers candidates with proficiency in Microsoft Word and Excel. Both temporary and permanent placements. All fees employer paid.

Pro Staff
11100 N.E. 8th, #140
Bellevue WA 98004
(425) 453-8216
Fax: (425) 453-8337
http://www.prostaff.com

Pro Temps
17317 139th Ave. N.E.
Woodinville WA 98072
(425) 806-8000
Fax: (425) 806-8008
Specializes in placing people age 50 and older. Positions range from clerical to administrative support to controller, operations manager and project manager. Few entry-level opportunities. Pay: $8 an hour to $60,000. Temporary, temp-to-hire and permanent. To apply, you'll need both personal and professional references

and a resume (two pages maximum). Many positions require that you keyboard at least 50 words per minute and are proficient in Word and Excel. Many also require 10-key by touch. Receptionist positions require proficiency with multi-line telephone systems. Makes placements from Kent to Arlington. Local firm, established in 1996.

Public Schools Personnel Cooperative
601 McPhee Rd. S.W.
Olympia WA 98502
(360) 753-2855
Jobline: (360) 664-2058
Substitute service (certified): (360) 753-3270
Substitute services (classified): (360) 753-2855
Fax: (360) 664-2057
http://www.esd113.wednet.edu/personnel/
Contact: Laura Barckley, director
Posts openings and accepts applications for Educational Service District 113; for certified (teaching) positions in 11 south Puget Sound school districts; and for classified (support and technical) jobs in four of the same districts . Interviews are scheduled and conducted by districts with openings. The job application form is online, although you must print it out and mail it in with other materials (such as proof of certification).

Quick Labor
10334 Aurora Ave. N.
Seattle WA 98133
(206) 522-9135
Fax: (206) 522-9135
Contact: Devin Smith, manager
Provides temporary workers for assembly, warehouse, landscaping, construction and demolition jobs. Applicants can walk in, preferably the day before they want to work. Work is assigned starting at 5:30 a.m.

Remedy Intelligent Staffing
601 Union St., #1707
Seattle WA 98101
(206) 223-0747
Fax: (206) 223-0981
aaseattle@remedystaff.com
A franchise headquartered in California. Offers temporary and permanent placements; you can register at one office and work from several. Provides clerical and administrative (to administrative assistant), technical (help desk support), customer service and light industrial staff. Candidates should have proficiency with Microsoft Word and Excel, keyboard 40 words per minute and have a year's experience. You'll also need a professional appearance, even when applying at the agency. To apply, call for an appointment; it'll take two to four hours for the interview and tests. All fees employer paid.

Remedy Intelligent Staffing
6729 Ft. Dent Way, #225
Tukwila WA 98188
(206) 242-8016
Fax: (206) 242-9640
aatukwila@remedystaff.com

Remedy Intelligent Staffing
10900 N.E. 4th St., #1130
Bellevue WA 98004
(425) 453-8017
Fax: (425) 637-1313
aabellevue@remedystaff.com

Remedy Intelligent Staffing
19203 36th Ave. W., #104
Lynnwood WA 98036
(425) 771-5431
Fax: (425) 774-5882
aalynnwood@remedystaff.com

ReproTemps
320 108th N.E., #600
Bellevue WA 98004
(425) 451-3883
Affiliated with Garden Variety Personnel. Specializes in printing and copy center jobs. Prefers applicants to have at least a year of recent, full-time experience in the industry.

Re:sources Connection LLC
See Deloitte & Touche Re:sources Connection LLC.

Robert Half International
601 Union St., #4300
Seattle WA 98101
(206) 749-0960
Fax: (206) 749-9243
http://www.roberthalf.com
seattle@roberthalf.com
Focus: permanent placements in MIS, accounting and finance, including such positions as bookkeeper, tax manager, CIO and CFO. Prefers candidates to have at least two years of experience. All fees employer paid.

City of Seattle
Special Employment Programs
710 Second Ave., 12th floor
Seattle WA 98104-1793
(206) 684-7986
Fax: (206) 684-5809
Refers workers to temporary positions in city departments. Most jobs are full-time

for a month or more; most openings are in office support. You'll be easier to place if you have a year or more experience in an office, can keyboard at least 50 words per minute and are proficient with Word for Windows, Excel and database management programs. Pay range: $9.94-$14 an hour, with the most common positions paying $11.82 and $13.02 an hour.

Senior Staffing
15 S. Grady Way, #321
Renton WA 98055
(425) 204-9509, toll-free: (888) SR-STAFF
Fax: (425) 204-9519
deand@ix.netcom.com
Contact: Dean Dorcas, president
Specializes in, but does not limit its placements to, those 50 and older. About 70 per cent of the placements from this office are temp-to-hire; the balance are long-term temporary. Pays at least $7.50 an hour for customer service, reception, bookkeeping and sales jobs; call center jobs (both inbound and outboard calls, but most of a non-sales nature) pay $7.50-$9.50. Light industrial assignments pay $6.75-$8. In late 1997 opened a Puyallup office:

Senior Staffing Inc.
11803 100th Ave. Ct. E., #102
Puyallup WA 98373
(253) 472-9944
Contact: Jim Naeher, branch manager
Focus: similar to Renton office excluding call center work. Pay range is slightly lower.

Snelling Personnel Services
4300 S. Pine St., #91
Tacoma WA 98409
(253) 473-1800; from Seattle: (206) 244-0204
Contact: Lee Janssen, manager
A franchise that handles many Seattle (rather than Tacoma) jobs in engineering, data processing, clerical and sales. Some fees are paid by the job-seeker.

Snelling Personnel Services
15 S. Grady Way, #246
Renton WA 98055
(425) 228-6500; from Bellevue: (425) 455-3117; from Seattle: (206) 621-7967
Fax: (425) 228-8661
snelling15@aol.com
Contact: Joan Dubie
A franchise, but not otherwise affiliated with other Snelling offices. Same owner since 1969. Focus: light industrial and administrative (general office to office manager) on a temporary or permanent basis. Also handles contract engineering jobs. Application procedures: for light industrial, call for walk-in interview schedule; for administrative, fax a resume or call for an appointment (allow an hour to 90 minutes for your interview and test); and for engineering, fax a resume. All fees employer paid.

Snelling Personnel Services
2101 Fourth Ave., #1330
Seattle WA 98121
(206) 441-8895
Fax: (206) 448-5373
http://www.snelling.com/Seattle
snelling@serv.net
Contact: Sue Truscott
A franchise providing temporary and permanent placements in office services, accounting and finance, sales, information systems and light industrial.

SOS Staffing Services Inc.
2110 116th Ave. N.E., #E
Bellevue WA 98004
(425) 462-8450
Fax: (425) 462-8655
http://www.sosstaffing.com
Contact: Collienne Becker, placement specialist
Handles temporary and temp-to-hire placements for administrative, technical and light industrial jobs ranging from call center sales to executive secretary, legal secretary and electronic technician. A branch of a Utah company, with an additional Northwest office expected in early 1998. To apply, call for an appointment; allow 90 minutes for your interview and test. All fees employer paid.

Staffing Resources
1000 Second Ave., #1700
Seattle WA 98104
(206) 583-2711
Fax: (206) 583-2725
kimbell@aol.com
Contact: Kim Martin, staffing specialist
Part of the Florida-based Accustaff. Handles temporary and permanent placements in adminstrative, legal (as senior as attorneys) and accounting (including controllers). Prefers that candidates are proficient in Microsoft Office and, for legal jobs, WordPerfect. Also prefers a stable work history (one to three years in the most recent organizations). Resumes should be scannable. All fees employer paid. Makes placements from Renton to Everett from this and its two other offices:

Staffing Resources
320 108th Ave. N.E., #504
P.O. Box 50070
Bellevue WA 98015
(425) 451-7886
Fax: (425) 462-5752

Staffing Resources
15 S. Grady Way, #422
Renton WA 98055
(425) 204-9466
Fax: (425) 204-1411

TAD Resources International, Inc.
15 S. Grady Way, #509
Renton WA 98055
(425) 226-8333, (800) 532-0368
Fax:(425) 226-8374
http://www.tadseattle.com
jobs@tadseattle.com
This firm has three local offices, with all contract technical jobs—engineers, drafters, software professionals—being placed from this location. Two other offices handle clerical and light industrial positions:

TAD Resources International, Inc.
631 Strander Blvd., Bldg. A, #D
Tukwila WA 98188
(206) 575-3888
Fax: (206) 575-0932
http://www.tadseattle.com
Focus: temporary clerical and light industrial work. All fees employer paid.

TAD Resources International, Inc.
2849 152nd Ave., Bldg. 9, #B
Redmond WA 98052
(425) 861-7671
Fax: (425) 861-6876
http://www.tadseattle.com
Focus: temporary clerical and light industrial work. All fees employer paid.

Temporarily Yours
1000 Second Ave., #3550
Seattle WA 98104
(206) 386-5400
Fax: (206) 386-4809
Specializes in temporary and temp-to-hire positions in administrative support, from file clerk to executive secretary and executive assistent. Most openings are for receptionist/word processors, who need experience with a busy multi-line (at least six- to 12-line) phone system, Microsoft Office, good customer service skills, poise and a commitment to stay in the receptionist position. Such a candidate can make $7.50-$9.50 an hour on a temporary basis, $20,000-$25,000 on a permanent basis. To apply, call for an appointment; allow two hours for your interview and test. Bring along a resume that details skills relevant to the job you seek. Serves clients from the Kent Valley to Lynnwood, including Preston. You can register at either office. All fees employer paid.

Temporarily Yours
10655 N.E. 4th, #500
Bellevue WA 98004
(425) 646-6610
Fax: (425) 646-9730

Terra Personnel Group

8625 Evergreen Way, #203
Everett WA 98208
(425) 355-7223; from Seattle: (206) 745-5141; toll-free: (800) 755-7638
Fax: (425) 353-1612
http://www.terrasvc.com
resume@terrasvc.com
A local firm established in 1983. Affiliated with LegalStaff and Terra Technical
Services. Terra Temporary Services places administrative support, light industrial
and assembly workers. For some jobs, those at least 16 can be hired. Positions
range from entry-level to experienced. You can apply by calling for an appointment or by sending in a resume. When you register, you'll need two references. All
fees employer paid.

Today's Temporary

1501 Fourth Ave., #2045
Seattle WA 98101
(206) 467-1054
Fax: (206) 467-1832
http://www.todays.com
Contact: Linda Legg, operations manager
Handles temporary and temp-to-hire placement of administrative support, legal
support (to legal secretary), accounting support (including accounts payable and
accounts receivable clerks) and insurance staff (including claims adjusters, adju-
dicators, claims processors/member services). To apply, you must be at least 18
and have at least three months office experience, two professional references, a
telephone and reliable transportation (public or private). You'll be easier to place
if you are proficient in Microsoft Office and for some legal jobs, WordPerfect.
Accounting candidates need experience with function-specific software such as
QuickBooks. Pay ranges from $7 an hour for a clerk to $20 an hour for an executive
secretary. All fees are employer paid. To apply, contact either this or the Bellevue
office.

Today's Temporary

10900 N.E. 8th St., #614
Bellevue WA 98004
(425) 455-9090
Fax: (425) 455-8469

Total Staffing Solutions

1001 Fourth Ave. Plaza, #3200
Seattle WA 98154
(206) 682-7266
Fax: (206) 682-7227
Headquartered in Maryland. This branch handles temporary light industrial and
clerical assignments. Clients are in Seattle, south King County and on the Eastside.
To apply, call for an appointment; allow at least an hour for your interview and
tests. All fees employer paid.

Transitions

1120 E. Terrace, #300
Seattle WA 98122
(206) 320-1266
Fax: (206) 325-5478
A local firm established in 1996. Handles entry-level and professional positions in technical (for example, mechanical engineer or programmer), medical (including medical assistant and physician assistant), clerical and light industrial fields. Temporary and permanent. To apply, call for an appointment or walk in; allow 90 minutes for your interview and test. All fees employer paid.

Uniforce Services

40 Lake Bellevue Dr., #123
Bellevue WA 98005
(425) 646-8003
Fax: (425) 646-0198
Contact: John Soth, general manager
A franchise operation of a national firm. Temporary placement of administrative support staff (including word processors, data entry clerks and executive assistants) and graphic designers and illustrators. Office jobs require good computer skills, including Microsoft Office; they pay $8-16 an hour. Graphics positions require proficiency with programs such as PageMaker, Photoshop and Illustrator, usually on a PC; they pay $16 an hour and more. All fees employer paid.

University of Washington

Temporary Services
1320 N.E. Campus Pkwy.
Seattle WA 98105
(206) 543-5813
Jobline: (206) 543-5420
An in-house temp agency, which fills clerical positions in UW offices on the main campus (about 20 per cent), at the UW medical center, Harborview Medical Center or in the south campus Health Sciences complex (about 60 per cent), near Northgate, on Capitol Hill or in branch campuses in Tacoma or Bothell. Does not handle grounds maintenance, skilled trades or academic positions. It's easier to be placed if you have good word processing, spreadsheet and dictating machine skills and can type more than 55 words per minute. Frequent openings for medical transcriptionists and those experienced with UW billing systems. Also has cashiering, food service, warehouse, mail sorting and theater ushering positions. Note: UTS receives about 350 applications a month and is able to interview about 20 per cent of applicants. No fee to applicants.

Volt Services Group

Headquartered in Orange, Calif., this employment agency has five divisions in the Seattle area. Besides Volt Engineering and Technical Services (see *Contract Employment*), they include:

Volt Accounting Specialists
1001 Fourth Ave., #2340
Seattle WA 98154
(206) 292-4393
Fax: (206) 292-9474
sea-vas@ix.netcom.com
Places accounting staff on a temporary, temp-to-hire and permanent basis. Positions range from accounts payable and accounts receivable clerks to controllers. To apply, call for an appointment. All fees employer paid.

Volt Accounting Specialists
600 108th Ave. N.E., #315
Bellevue WA 98004
(425) 451-9779
Fax: (425) 452-9851

Volt Services
1501 Fourth Ave., #1820
Seattle WA 98101
(206) 441-2929
Fax: (206) 292-4888
Places clerical, customer service and light industrial workers on a temporary, temp-to-hire and permanent basis. All fees employer paid.

Volt Services
600 108th Ave. N.E., #505
Bellevue WA 98004
(425) 451-9776
Fax: (425) 451-9796
Clerical applicants should call for appointments. Light industrial workers can walk in at noon; five interviews are conducted each afternoon. All fees employer paid.

Volt Services
15 S. Grady Way, #106
Renton WA 98055-3288
(425) 255-1271
Fax: (425) 228-0477
Clerical applicants should call for appointments. Light industrial and assembly applicants can walk in at 1:30 p.m. Monday-Thursday. All fees employer paid.

Volt Services
1133 164th St. S.W., #108
Lynnwood WA 98037
(425) 742-6161
Fax: (425) 745-9760

Volt Services
3700 Pacific Hwy E., #107
Tacoma WA 98424
(253) 922-7411
Fax: (253) 922-7515

Warehouse Demo Services

330 Fourth St.
Kirkland WA 98033
(425) 889-0797
Fax: (425) 828-3845
Contact: Sheri van der Voort, human resources director
Looking for a seasonal or permanent part-time job? Able to stand six hours on concrete floors? This firm handles product demonstrators for Costco warehouse stores in nine western states, including 18 in Washington. Most demonstrators work two to four days a week, with the six-hour shifts almost always including weekends. Each warehouse employs 30-50 demonstrators, with additional staff hired for the holiday season. Pay is based on location and starts at $6.77-$7.25 an hour. Applicants should be energetic, strong, friendly and have a customer service orientation. To apply, stop at the Costco where you'd like to work and ask for the warehouse demo service supervisor.

WesTech

1200 112th Ave. N.E., #C-110
Bellevue WA 98004
(425) 451-3848
Fax: (425) 637-9793
Places engineering, computer software and manufacturing production staff on a temporary, temp-to-hire and contract basis. Engineering positions include technical writers and illustrators, technicians, drafters, designers and electrical, mechanical, structural, civil, aerospace and chemical engineers. Hourly pay varies from $28-$40 for entry-level engineers to $60-$80 for senior professionals. Computer jobs range from help desk to programmers; candidates should have completed a certification program or a college degree or have significant experience. A recent computer science graduate might earn $35,000-$45,000. Most manufacturing production positions are for skilled workers and professionals rather than managers. An assembler can make $7.50-$12 an hour. Because some entry-level positions don't require much communication, they are apppropriate for candidates with limited English skills. A technician, especially a graduate of a two-year technical program, can start at $9-$11 an hour and eventually make as much as $20 an hour. To apply, call for a telephone screening or fax in your resume with a letter indicating the kind of job you seek. Affiliated with Nu West. All fees employer paid.

Woods & Associates

1221 Second Ave., #430
Seattle WA 98101
(206) 623-2930
Fax: (206) 623-1216
A local firm established in 1987. Places administrative staff in legal, financial and health care support positions. Paralegals are usually the highest level positions filled. Placements may be temporary, contract or permanent. To apply, call for an appointment, which may take 90 minutes or more. All fees employer paid.

9. Career Transition Help:
What's Right for You?

What's a career counselor?

How does counseling differ from outplacement?

What's "career guidance" and "executive marketing"?

How much do these services cost?

How can you determine which of these programs are appropriate and cost-effective supplements to your own job-search efforts?

This chapter briefly explains several career assistance programs, what credentials are required of career advisers and the fees you might be expected to pay. Most important, this chapter is intended to clarify that none of these programs provide placement.

A counseling agency or career marketer's ad may say, "We help you find the best job," but neither a career counselor nor an outplacement program introduces you to employers or gives you exclusive access to job openings. As the National Career Development Association (NCDA) warns, be wary of services that promise more money, better jobs, faster responses to your resume or an immediate solution to a career problem. A formal career transition program can help you define your career and life goals, identify transferrable skills, revise your resume and improve your interviewing skills, but it cannot find you a job.

CAREER COUNSELORS

Career counselors often hold graduate degrees in psychology, counseling or related fields. Some have worked in college career or advising centers, others in outplacement. However, Washington has no education or experience requirements; according to the state Department of Health's Counselor Program, which registers only mental health counselors, you can charge for your counseling services after you've done nothing more than paid a $40 registration fee and completed a four-hour HIV/AIDS course.

Only a handful of professionals across the state are National Certified Career Counselors, a credential awarded to those with graduate degrees in counseling and extensive work experience who've passed exams created by the National Board for Certified Counselors.

Another common counseling service—administration and interpretation of the results of such popular career advising tests as the Myers-Briggs Type Indicator and Strong Interest Inventory (formerly the Strong Campbell)—is controlled by the tests' publisher, who restrict distribution of the tests to those who have completed either a class in psychological testing and measurement or the publisher's own certification programs.

What does this mean? That in this state anyone can call himself or herself a career counselor. The Yellow Pages listing for "career counseling" also includes businesses and individuals that may be related to the job search, but are not counselors. (For example, that's where the company that publishes this book and other job-search guides is listed in the telephone directory.)

Now let's talk about what career counselors can do. Counselors in private practice may charge $50, $75 or more an hour to help you clarify life or career goals or prepare you for a specific job search. As the NCDA points out, a counselor may administer and interpret tests and inventories such as the Myers-Briggs, give you career exploration assignments and help you improve your decision-making skills. Or your counselor may work on strengthening your resume, interview skills and negotiating ability.

Career counseling also is available through many nonprofits and colleges, often at more economical rates than those offered by private counselors. At Bellevue Community College (425-641-2215), for example, taking the Myers-Briggs and Strong Interest Inventory costs just $10 per test; for interpretation of test results, community members are referred to a private counselor who charges about $70 a session. If you're a student (even if you're enrolled in just one class), you'll pay even less for the tests and you'll pay nothing at all for the interpretation by a BCC on-site counselor. At Olympic College in Bremerton (360-478-4702), many job-search and resume workshops are free. Similar programs are offered through YWCAs, public libraries, military bases' family service centers, professional associations and the alumni career services programs at many universities and graduate schools.

If you're considering a career counselor, look first for low-cost or free introductions to the counselors you're considering. Read their books, attend their free presentations at local bookstores and libraries, and sign up for their workshops at community colleges and professional association meetings. Many counselors work part-time with colleges and universities, so you can enroll in a low-cost class and then, if you're comfortable with the counselor, continue with private counseling. For help in evaluating counseling programs, check with the NCDA (888-326-1750, http://www.ncda1.org) and the Puget Sound Career Development Association (http://www.pscda.com), which on its web site offers an article by local counselor Larry Gaffin, "Choosing the Right Career Services for You."

RETAIL OUTPLACEMENT SERVICES

Outplacement is a service often provided by employers when they fire or lay off staff. Traditionally, outplacement services were offered only to very senior management, almost always on an individual basis. However, in recent years some employers have begun providing career transition or "re-employment" assistance to many employees when mergers, unit closures and general downsizing result in huge layoffs. In these cases, it's more typical for staff and middle managers to be provided help as a group.

There is no licensing or other regulation of outplacement firms. Although some local firms were established by or employ career counselors, that is not a requirement. Outplacement, both "corporate" and "retail", might be provided by people who've worked in personnel or in career placement centers or by "graduates" of the the same company's outplacement program.

In contrast to "corporate outplacement" is "retail outplacement." You'll often see ads for this service under headings such as "career guidance", "career marketing" and "executive marketing" in newspapers' employment advertising sections. The services are similar, but while "corporate outplacement" is employer-paid, "retail outplacement" services are paid for by the job-seeker.

Most providers of retail outplacement services in the Seattle area are reluctant to quote fees, saying their charges varied depending on the job-seeker's needs. However, some firms cited fees starting at $1,000-$5,000 and going to $6,000-$10,000. (One firm outside the state advertises an eight-hour job-search workshop for $2,500 plus meals, lodging and travel.) For a highly-compensated individual, fees are sometimes based on the salary you seek or the most recent salary you've made. Fees often must be paid in full when you contract for help.

Retail outplacement is typically provided as a package; occasionally it can be purchased on a per-hour or per-workshop basis. The package may include resume writing, coaching, videotaping of mock interviews and access to the retail outplacement firm's databases of local employers and search firms. Some outplacement firms include "candidate biographies" on their web sites. Some firms offer selected services, such as a resume revision or short-term counseling, on an hourly basis (one firm's fee: $200 an hour).

A package of career transition services, including a self-marketing workshop, office space and access to computers, the Internet and fax machines, is also available through Forty Plus of Puget Sound (425-450-0040, 40plus-wa@halcyon.com), the local chapter of a national nonprofit membership group for those aged 40 and older who have made $40,000 or more. The initiation fee is $495; in addition, there's a $50 monthly fee and a volunteer work requirement.

Considering paying for retail outplacement or "career marketing"? First, carefully evaluate what you need: resume and cover letter help, perhaps, or help with interviewing and negotiating skills; a support group, employer directories and databases, and trade journals; or a temporary office and Internet access. Determine if what you need most is available through an outplacement program and how the costs compare with similar resources elsewhere. Consider the quality of the outplacement program; if possible, talk to colleagues who've used this or other programs.

10. Job Bulletins and Resume Listings

Whether you're researching a specific function or industry or looking for a place to post your resume, this chapter provides information on several resources. Most are local and many are available free, especially if you have access to the Internet. This chapter also suggests how to locate other job-search resources. For additional help, see *Internet Resources for Your Job Search* and *Using Professional and Alumni Associations*.

JOB BULLETINS AND LISTINGS

WORK
http://www.wa.gov/esd/jstart.htm
A State of Washington site that's part of the WORK job/job-seeker database. This site allows you to research open positions, both in government and private industry. For the resume database site, see the last page of this chapter.

University of Washington Job Bulletins
Center for Career Services
301 Loew Hall
Box 352190, University of Washington
Seattle WA 98195
(206) 543-9104
http://weber.u.washington.edu/~careers/joblist.html
Issued weekly (biweekly during Autumn Quarter), Bulletin #1 includes K-12 teaching, support services and administrative positions. Issued weekly throughout the year, #2 covers career positions in business, industry and the public sector. Most listings are for the Northwest. Each bulletin costs $50 per academic quarter. The UW also has a 24-hour jobline that, for an additional $50 fee per quarter, allows you to access all of the job openings listed with the center.

Washington State University Online Job Listings
Career Services
Lighty Building, Room 180, Washington State University
Pullman WA 99164-1061
(509) 335-9107
http://www.wsu.edu/csweb/jobs.html
Online listings of jobs for graduating students and alumni in business, education, government, nonprofits. Also lists internships, student jobs, and advanced and special-study opportunities. Listings from across the U.S.

Western Washington University Job Opportunity Bulletin
Career Resources Center
Western Washington University
Bellingham WA 98225-9002
(360) 650-2980
http://www.wwu.edu/~careers
You can select from the following categories: business, industry, government and nonprofits; higher education; elementary education; school administration; secondary education; special educational services; and internships. Each is published weekly except for internships, issued on alternate weeks. An estimated 85 per cent of the job listings are along the Interstate 5 corridor. Cost (lower fees for alumni): $10 processing per year plus $40 per category for a four-month subscription.

Central Washington University Bulletins
Career Development Services
Central Washington University
400 E. 8th St.
Ellensburg WA 98926-7499
(509) 963-1921, 963-2404
http://www.cwu.edu/~careerdv/home.htmlx
Issues a six-part job bulletin weekly (or as infrequently as monthly when fewer openings are received). You can select from levels (lists) of openings in business or education. Most jobs are in Washington. Cost (lower fees for alumni): $50 processing per year plus $25 per level for a four-month mail or e-mail subscription.

RSVP Washington
(800) 963-RSVP
Fax: (509) 963-2560
rsvpwa@cwu.edu
Physically located at CWU Career Development Services (see above), this is a state-funded program database of jobs and job-seekers for special education positions in public schools. Once registered, job-seekers can access listings of openings and have contact information for themselves sent directly to districts with openings. Job-seekers also get a bulletin listing the openings. No charge to job-seekers or districts.

Seattle Pacific University Education Vacancy Bulletin
Career Development Center
Seattle Pacific University
Seattle WA 98119
(206) 281-2018
http://www.spu.edu/cdc/newindex.html
Lists openings for certified K-12 teachers and administrators. Published weekly February-October. Subcription: $35 per quarter, with lower rates for SPU students and alumni.

Washington Education Association Position Listing Service
Washington Education Association
33434 8th S.
Federal Way WA 98003
(253) 941-6700, (800) 622-3393
http://www.wa.nea.org/Jobline/JOBLIST.HTM
Job openings for administrators, teachers and support and maintenance staff in
Northwest schools and colleges. Some positions (a community college webmaster
or HR director, for example) do not require education credentials. A three-month
mail subscription is $10 for WEA members, $35 for nonmembers; on the web, it's
free.

Job Net
Association of Washington Cities
1076 Franklin St. S.E.
Olympia WA 98501
(360) 753-4137
http://www.mrsc.org/awcfiles/class.htm
Monthly listing of municipal managerial and professional positions (from entry
level to $120,000 a year). Cost for mailed bulletins: $8 for a six-month subscription
and $15 for a year.

Interchristo
19303 Fremont Ave. N.
Seattle WA 98133
(206) 546-7330
http://www.jobleads.org
dlh@crista.org
Contact: Denise Henderson, manager
Part of Crista Ministries. A job referral service that uses a job-seeker's preferences
to create a customized jobs bulletin. No placement help. Most positions are in
Christian nonprofits, from the volunteer to the executive level; 80 per cent of the
jobs require relocation. A three-month subscription costs $59.95.

Sound Opportunities
P.O. Box 16722
Seattle WA 98116
(206) 933-6556
Fax: (206) 933-6566
http://www.earthlink.net/~soundop
soundop@earthlink.net
Advertises openings in Washington and Oregon nonprofits. Distributed to placement offices, libraries, nonprofits and government agencies. Subscriptions to the
biweekly print bulletin: $16 for three months. After subscribers have been notified,
most jobs also appear on the web site.

NP-Jobs
Nurse Practitioner Support Services
(800) 467-7701
http://www.nurse.net/np/index2.html

Jobs for nurse practitioners and other advanced practice nurses. Issued biweekly. A 15-issue subscription by mail is $25. After subscribers have been notified, jobs also appear on the web site. Issued by a for-profit publisher.

Contract Employment Weekly
C.E. Publications
P.O. Box 3006
Bothell WA 98041-3006
(425) 806-5200
Fax: (425) 806-5585
http://www.ceweekly.wa.com
webmaster@ceweekly.com.
Used by contract service agencies to advertise temporary engineering and IT/IS jobs. The $65 annual subscription for mailed bulletins includes a directory of contract service firms. Electronic subscriptions are $30 a year. There's a $18, five-copy mail trial offer. Issued by a for-profit firm.

Engineering Central
http://www.engcen.com/index.html
Advertises permanent and contract engineering jobs across the U.S. You can access the list of openings at no charge.

Medscape Career Center
http://www. medscape.com
Advertises health care job listings across the U.S. through the Monster Board (see *Internet Resources for Your Job Search*).

First Employment Listing Services, Inc.
14900 Interurban Ave.
Tukwila WA 98168
(206) 439-1000
Fax: (206) 439-6449
A branch of a for-profit firm headquartered in Michigan. Job-seekers can subscribe to a job directory, which includes job openings employers have reported to First Employment. No placement services. All fees are paid by the job seeker.

RESUME LISTINGS AND DATABASES

Here you'll find examples of services that help you market yourself. Those services that charge to include your resume are listed only if they are nonprofits. For-profit services are listed only if they charge no fees to job-seekers.

You can find other online resume databases by typing a phrase such as "resume database" into a search engine. Be aware, however, that such databases ordinarily charge fees to job-seekers. In late 1997, these fees ranged from $35 to several hundred dollars.

King County Nurses Association
4649 Sunnyside Ave. N., #224
Seattle WA 948103
(206) 545-0603
Fax: (206) 545-3558
http://www.kcna.org

kcna@kcna.org

An affiliate of the Washington State Nurses Association. Offers a nurse legal consultant clearinghouse, referring nurses to attorneys who need medical advice. KCNA members pay $20 each year to be listed, nonmembers $65. You need not be registered in Washington state to be listed.

Washington Contract Attorneys Group

14810 216th Ave. N.E.

Woodinville WA 98072

(206) 224-4459

Lawyers interested in working on a contract or temporary basis can join this group, which began as a spin-off of the state bar association's Lawyers' Assistance Program. Issues a quarterly directory (and monthly updates) of attorneys seeking contract work.

EthoSolutions Inc.

15815 S.E. 37th St., #104

Bellevue WA 98006-1825

(425) 957-7000

Fax: (425) 957-7133

http://www.jobspan.com

Specializing in health care (ranging from clinical to operations to finance, information systems and administration), this for-profit organization provides a candidate database that employers can use on a subscription basis. Job-seekers can complete a professional profile via the web site and be added to EthoSolutions' database at no charge. Listings are confidential and job-seekers can specify if certain employers should not have access to their files. Local; established in 1996.

Career Site

http://www.amcity.com/seattle

A free service of the online edition of the *Puget Sound Business Journal*, this employer/job-seeker database allows you to search positions by your criteria and then forward your resume to specific employers.

WORK

http://www.wa.gov/esd/tresume.html

http://www.wa.gov/esd/jstart.htm

These two State of Washington sites are part of the WORK job/job-seeker database. The first site allows you to post your credentials so that any employer can check them; the second site allows you to research open positions, both in government and private industry.

11. Internet Resources for Your Job Search

Why is the Internet important in your job search? First, because e-mail is today an important means of communicating with many recruiters and prospective employers. When you read this book's directories of recruiters and contract employers, you'll note how many placement professionals prefer to be contacted via e-mail.

Second, because Internet savvy sends a signal about your skills. If you can't use e-mail, if you don't have a resume available via e-mail or a diskette, some recruiters will perceive you to be out of sync in this technically sophisticated community.

Third, with the web you can—at any time of day, regardless of where you are—research an industry, a job function, an employer or a product or service. You can retrieve new and archived newspaper stories and use online forums to ask for others' opinions and references. You can network with long-lost classmates and former colleagues.

And you can access basic information: addresses and phone numbers, maps, ferry and flight schedules, cost-of-living indices, child care providers and current classified advertising for both employment and real estate.

This chapter provides an overview of Internet resources. Detailed listings of employer and professional association URLs are found in *How to Find a Good Job in Seattle*, also by Linda Carlson. Or use the search techniques described below.

For readers who do not have their own Internet access, this chapter also lists sites that offer computers with modems. This information is expected to change quickly; check fees, hours and availability prior to visiting an Internet lab.

Because many job-search resources are now available in both hard copy and online forms, some of the information in this chapter also appears in *Job Bulletins and Resume Listings*.

FOR INTERNET NOVICES

If you're a web novice, here's some suggestions on getting started.

First, to research a prospective employer, type its name in a search engine such as Alta Vista (http://www.altavista.digital.com). You may get thousands of references. However, if an organization has its own web site, that usually will be one of the first references shown by the search engine: http://www.microsoft.com, for example, or http://www.boeing.com. You may find recent press announcements, company history, product descriptions, job postings, online application forms and e-mail addresses for human resources or hiring managers' e-mail addresses on employers' own web sites.

Even employers without web sites may be mentioned in news stories that provide valuable background information for you. You can access these through a search engine or by searching the archives of publications with online files (the *Puget Sound Business Journal,* for example).

Second, check the local directories that provide links to employers' own web sites; one to try is http://www.edc-sea.org, the Economic Development Council's membership roster. For community and technical colleges, use http://www.ctc.edu. For government, use Municipal Research & Services Center, http://www.mrsc.org or Home Page Washington, http://www.wa.gov.

You also can use search engines to locate job advertisements, although specifying a level can be difficult. For example, if you search for "Seattle computer science jobs", you'll get more than 100 references, ranging from local employers' job listings to the mayor's most recent speech about jobs.

Many college career center sites provide valuable job-search information and link to other job-search sites. Start with the local universities' career sites (or your own alma mater's page) and you'll find information appropriate for almost any career level.

PUBLIC INTERNET ACCESS SITES

You don't have a computer? Or your computer doesn't have a modem? Or you're having trouble accessing the Internet? Here you'll find sites where you can go online for free or at modest rates. In addition, many of these computer labs offer Internet "how-to" classes or informal tutoring. For more help using the Internet, check your community college's catalog for a short noncredit class or workshop.

Career Development Center
(425) 271-0488
borc@seanet.com
This Renton center is sponsored by such agencies as Washington State Employment Security, the Seattle-King County Private Industry Council and Renton Technical College. Free. Internet lab open to all job seekers. Call for hours.

King County Library System
http://www.kcls.lib.wa.us
Occasional free Internet workshops; call Community Relations, (206) 684-6606. Dial-in Internet access requires a King County library card; call the Answer Line at (425) 462-9600, (800) 462-9600.

Kitsap Regional Library
Administration: (360) 377-7601
Information: (360) 405-9100; from Bainbridge Island, (206) 780-2102
http://www.kitsap.lib.wa.us
Offers Internet access and free e-mail to county residents with library cards.

Pierce County Library System
(253) 536-6500
http://pcl1.pcl.lib.wa.us
Dial-in access: (253) 536-6195, 536-6070, 536-6067
For information about Internet programs, call the Public Services or Public Information departments. There's public access at five branches: South Hill, Parkland-Spanaway, Lakewood, University Place and Peninsula.

Seattle Public Library
http://www.spl.lib.wa.us
Dial-in access: (206) 386-4140
Access the Internet via terminals in many branches. For free Internet training, call Quick Information (206-386-4636) for a class schedule.

Tacoma Public Library
(253) 591-5666
http://www.tpl.lib.wa.us
Offers dial-in access to its catalog and to certain databases. Internet access at the main, Moore and McCormick facilities.

Timberland Regional Library
Olympia branch: (360) 352-0595
http://www.timberland.lib.wa.us
Online tutorials: http://www.timberland.lib.wa.us/tutorials.htm
Offers Internet access at each branch.

Powerful Schools
(206) 722-5543
http://www.seattleantioch.edu/Students/jdobmeier/PShome.html
Computer lab access at Seattle's Hawthorne School 3-8 p.m. Open lab with training and tutors.

Forty Plus of Puget Sound
(425) 450-0040
40plus-wa@halcyon.com
Web access for members. See *Career Transition Help.*

Businesses offering computer terminals with Internet access include (fees vary):

The Virtual Commons, Seattle, (206) 281-7339

Capitol Hill Internet Cafe, Seattle, (206) 860-6858

The Speakeasy Cafe, Seattle, (206) 728-9770

Kinko's in most Puget Sound locations

HELP AT LOCAL UNIVERSITIES' SITES

Once you're online, an excellent starting point is a university web site. Most offer career advice (sometimes including help for those with years of experience) and links to web sites with more advice.

University of Washington Center for Career Services
http://weber.u.washington.edu/~careers/
Links to job-search resources, publications and companies' own web sites.

Washington State University Career Services
http://www.careers.wsu.edu
Besides the online listings of jobs for graduating students and alumni, internships,

student jobs, and advanced and special-study opportunities, the "Alumni Services" section offers help with resumes, cover letters and thank-you notes.

Western Washington University Career Resources Center
http://www.wwu.edu/~careers/joblink.html
Links to job listings, employment agencies and job-search web sites.

Central Washington University Career Development Services
http://www.cwu.edu/~careerdv/home.htmlx
Check the alumni section for advice on career issues and links to other sites.

Seattle Pacific University Career Development Center
http://www.spu.edu:80/depts/cdc/
This web site offers job-search advice and helpful links, including one to a cost-of-living calculator.

Seattle University Career Development Center
http://www.seattleu.edu/student/cdc
Provides links to job-search information.

Pacific Lutheran University Career Development
http://www.plu.edu/~career/
Provides job-search advice, joblines and links to job-search sites.

University of Puget Sound Academic and Career Advising
http://www.ups.edu/advising/Career.htm
Describes many different tests and inventories used in career advising and provides links to job-search sites.

Center for Deaf Students
http://www.sccd.ctc.edu/~ccdeafst
Oriented to the needs of deaf students enrolled at or graduated from Seattle Community College District programs. The "Deaf Community" option provides information on employment services and links to community services.

PROFESSIONAL ASSOCIATION SITES

Washington Education Association
http://www.wa.nea.org/Jobline/JOBLIST.HTM
The online Position Listing Service. Describes job openings for administrators, teachers and support and maintenance staff in Northwest schools and colleges. Free. Links to job postings at most state universities, teacher certification information, the office of the Superintendent of Public Instruction (which connects to web sites maintained by school districts and educational service districts), and to RSVP Washington (see *Job Bulletins and Resume Listings*).

Job Net
http://www.mrsc.org/awcfiles/class.htm
The Association of Washington Cities' monthly listing of municipal managerial and professional positions (from entry level to $120,000 a year).

Medical Marketing Association
http://www.mmanet.org
The national's site; includes job listings.

National Society of Fund Raising Executives
http://www.nsfre.org
The national's site. Links to *NonProfit Times*, which has job listings at http://www.nptimes.com/classified.html.

GOVERNMENT SITES

City of Seattle
http://www.ci.seattle.wa.us
For job-search advice and instructions on applying for City of Seattle positions, see http://www.ci.seattle.wa.us/personnel/jobs.htm. Also allows you to connect to other cities (from Bellevue and Bellingham to Tukwila, Tumwater, Vancouver and Yakima) by selecting from "Other Places." This link also works for several counties and Washington state's web site.

Washington State Employment Security
General: http://www.wa.gov/esd
WORK database: http://www.wa.gov/esd/resume.html
Job database: http://www.wa.gov/esd/jstart.htm
Advice: http://www.wa.gov/esd/1stop/
Allows you to post a resume that any employer can access or search a database of open positions. Information on electronic resume preparation. Wide variety of other career and job-search advice, with links to state's own executive recruiter (see *Executive Search Firms: Locally Based* and *Industry Specialists*). At http://www.wa.gov/features/wm_law.htm, "An Online Women's Roadmap to Careers in Law," you'll find information about women in law and helpful links. (No job listings in this area at press time, however.)

America's Job Bank
http://www.ajb.dni.us
Job listings sponsored by the U.S. Department of Labor and state employment offices. Can be searched by job type and location. Site provides job-search advice, including comments on preparing electronic and scannable resumes.

Securities and Exchange Commission
http://www.sec.gov
Through EDGAR, the federal government's Electronic Data Gathering Analysis and Retrieval system, you can access much (but not all) of the information filed by public companies. At a minimum, the information filed by a firm will include a brief description of the firm's business and market.

FreeEDGAR
http://www.freeedgar.com
Maintained by an Eastside firm, this privately owned site provides some sorting of SEC information. For example, it allows you to select only the documents most recently filed by a company.

PUBLICATIONS ON THE WEB

National Employment Business Weekly
http://www.nbew.com/
You can find this excellent Dow Jones publication on the newsstand or you can
check excerpts from past issues on the web site. The help wanted ads, which come
from the *Wall Street Journal*, appear only in the print publication.

Seattle Times
http://www.seattletimes.com.
http://www.seatimes.com
Besides summaries of top stories, provides real estate and help wanted advertising.
The real estate section includes a mortgage payment calculator and links to any real
estate brokers sponsoring the online edition.

Seattle Post-Intelligencer
http://www.seattlep-i.com
Accesses the same advertising as the *Seattle Times*. Also provides news headlines
from the P-I and, through NewsWorks (http://www.newsworks.com), from many
papers across the U.S.

Puget Sound Business Journal
http://www.amcity.com/seattle
Offers excerpts from the current week's issue and an archive of recent stories.
Links to 35 other business weeklies owned by the same company. Includes "Career
Site," a free employer/job-seeker database that allows you to search positions by
your criteria and then forward your resume to specific employers.

Daily Journal of Commerce
http://www.djc.com
Seattle's daily business paper offers online excerpts; to access some stories, you
must be a subscriber.

Washington CEO
http://www.waceo.com
The online edition of this monthly on Washington business. Includes archives
starting with the May, 1995 issue.

Hoover's Online
http://www.hoovers.com
A well-known tool for researching companies, but most access is restricted to
subscribers.

Media Inc.
http://www.media-inc.com
Both Washington and Oregon job openings in the media, in advertising and in film
production are included on this monthly's web site.

Philanthropy Journal Online
http://www.philanthropy-journal.org/
Allows you search its files of job openings by geographic area; at press time, there
were six jobs listed for the Seattle area.

RELOCATION INFORMATION ON THE WEB

Greater Seattle Chamber of Commerce

http://www.seattlechamber.com

Sells a relocation packet, employer directories and job-search publications (including this book). "Moving to Seattle" links to local newspapers' advertising and to job postings from state, city and county government as well as businesses, schools and colleges. Provides a list of employer joblines.

Northwest Multiple Listing Service

http://www.nwrealestate.com

Nine western Washington multiple listing services work together to provide this listing of homes for sale. You can search by your specifications (geographical area, sales price, size, etc.).

The Homebuyer's Fair

http://www.homefair.com/home/

Provides a salary calculator to help you estimate how compensation in one city compares to what's needed in another part of the U.S. (or even overseas). For example, according to its calculator, if you're making $100,000 in Boston, you'll need $80,600 in Seattle; if you're moving from Des Moines, Iowa to Tacoma, you'll need $97,600...but if you're relocating from Des Moines to Bellevue, you'll want at least $105,000. Another feature, "The Insurance Professor," helps you estimate how relocation will impact your car insurance. (If you're paying $600 every six months in Des Moines, for example, you may pay $900-$1,300 in Tacoma.)

The Monster Board Relocation Service

http://www.monsterboard.com

Allows you to search for apartments by location, size, price and amenities.

Child Care Resources

http://www.wolfe.net/~most/ccr.htm

Provides a database of King County child care centers as well as programs for school-age children.

Riderlink

http://transit.metrokc.gov/

The King County web site provides information on public transportation within this county and, through Riderlink, connects you with web sites for bus travel in Everett and Kitsap and Pierce counties. Also links to ferry and Amtrak schedules.

PLACEMENT HELP ON THE INTERNET

Need some resume advice? Looking for salary data? Want to know what questions a headhunter is likely to ask? If you're online, advice is just a few keystrokes away.

What's to remember about information on the web? First, it may not be accurate. Today almost anyone can post almost anything on the Internet; there's no requirement that information be verified or edited for bias. Or the information may be accurate in its geographic area or industry, but not reflective of the job market in the Seattle area. (One example: a professional association's site offers advice from a southeastern firm on cover letters, recommending a two-column format that compares what an employer says it wants and the job-seeker's skills. In Seattle, however, this format is often criticized by employers.)

Information on the Internet also may be out-of-date. Once created, web sites sometimes are forgotten. Or they may be updated frequently, with old articles deleted to make room for new. Check your favorite sites for archives and key-word search functions to find older material.

With these warnings, here's some suggestions for finding online assistance. First, use your search engines to research topics such as "resumes", "cover letters", "interviews" and "joblines." A recent search turned up several references, including advice from the University of Chicago Business School career center, the *New York Times* and *USA Today*.

Second, as noted elsewhere, see what links are offered from professional association and college career center sites. Third, look at web sites provided by placement firms. For example:

Executive recruiters Kincannon & Reed (http://www.krsearch.com) offer links to professional associations related to their industry specialties.

Retained search firm Egon Zehnder International (http://www.zehnder.com/how.html) offers an article entitled, "How to Make the Executive Search Process Work for You in Your Job Search."

Another search firm, Ray & Berndtson (http://www.prb.com/html/intfaqs.htm), offers "Interviewing FAQs" to help you prepare for interviews.

The Association of Executive Search Consultants has a similar article on questions at http://www.interviewedge.com/news_views/4q93/5Intrv.html.

And James Kennedy, the publisher of *Executive Recruiter News*, provides "13 Tips on Responding to Executive Recruiters" (http://www.kennedyinfo.com/13tips.htm).

For job-search Q & A from executive search consultants Christian & Timbers, see "Expert Advice" at http://www.ctnet.com

Local technical recruiter Northwest Professional Management Services offers suggestions for the computer industry resume at http://www.nwproman.com.

Besides the resources provided by Puget Sound libraries, check the extensive files maintained by other libraries: for example, a regional library agency in northern California sponsors "Jobsmart" (http://jobsmart.org), which provides salary information, both national as well as California-specific.

For help creating a scannable resume, see Resumix's site, http://www.resumix.com. This firm, which has sold its scanning software to many Northwest employers, provides resume advice and a template for an online or scannable resume at "Creating Your Resume."

ROAD MAPS TO ADDITIONAL RESOURCES

"What Color Is Your Parachute"

http://www.washingtonpost.com/parachute
Hosted by the *Washington Post*, this site promotes books by "Parachute" author Richard Nelson Bolles and links to many other career sites.

CareerMosaic

http://www.careermosaic.com
Allows you to post a resume, search a jobs database and, through the "Career

Resource Center," get more job-search advice.

CareerNet
http://www.careers.org
One of many services is a directory of career resources with appropriate links sorted by city.

JobTrak
http://www.jobtrak.com
Oriented to college students and recent graduates, this service offers job listings, but to access them, you'll need a password from your school or alma mater. "Resource Center" links to other pages, including Hospitality Net's "Virtual Job Exchange", which is a job and resume database for the hospitality industry.

The Monster Board
http://www.monsterboard.com
The Career Search option allows you to check for job openings by geographic area; at press time, there were 200 in western Washington, ranging from mortgage loan officer and pharmacist, accountant and computer tech to software test engineer. "News Groups" shows search firms' openings.

12. Using Professional and Alumni Associations

Looking for jobs that may not be advertised widely? Looking for jobs that may not be advertised at all? Looking for a place to create a job?

Then look to professional and trade associations, both local and national, that serve your function and industry or the functions and industries you're considering.

Professional associations offer several services; for example, they may sell membership directories that provide contacts for a networking or cold calling campaign. Those who sell directories to nonmembers include the local chapters of the American Institute of Architects, the Washington Biotechnology and Biomedical Association, the Washington Society of Association Executives and the Washington Software & Digital Media Alliance.

Other groups will summarize job-seekers' objectives and experience in their newsletters, either free or at a very low cost. A few examples: the Pacific Northwest Newspaper Association, the Associated General Contractors and Professional Geographers of Puget Sound.

A detailed list of hundreds of professional associations, with local contacts, is included in *How To Find A Good Job In Seattle,* available from the publisher of this book. Or check Tracy Schneider's *Guide to Business-Related Organizations in Puget Sound* (call 206-935-9283) or your library's copy of the *Encyclopedia of Associations*, a Gale publication. Many professional associations now maintain web sites with local contact information (for how-to help, refer back to *Internet Resources for Your Job Search*).

When you're relocating, reviving a network or considering a career change, you can make valuable contacts through alumni associations and the alumni career services programs of your university or graduate school (sometimes offered through alumni associations, sometimes through campus career centers).

Services range from alumni directories (now often online) and alumni e-mail systems to job-search workshops and job bulletins circulated only to alumni. At some colleges, alumni can take career interest inventories and tests like the Myers-Briggs for free or for very modest fees. Some schools also have organized networks of alumni willing to provide information interviews and mentoring.

Both professional and alumni associations can introduce you to experienced professionals and managers in your field, people you might otherwise be unlikely to meet. However, remember that most of the people you meet through associations are volunteers. To assist you, they're taking time from their businesses. To ensure that you make good use of the few minutes you'll have together, do some homework so you're focused and have prepared appropriate questions. When you attend a meeting, it's your responsibility to introduce yourself and discreetly clarify your purpose. Passing out resumes over luncheon is not recommended, but you can collect business cards and make followup calls to those who invite you to telephone.

When you're networking, whether it's through associations or with referrals from colleagues and friends, don't let yourself get too busy for good manners. If you're invited to meet with someone over a meal, make sure you pick up the tab. Ask for help tactfully; regardless of your level, it is not appropriate to make demands such as, "This is what I need you to do for me." Don't expect people you've just met to give you unlimited access to their Rolodexes or to company or association directories.

Write a thank you note for each in-person meeting and for telephone conversations that extend more than a few minutes. When someone refers you to another networking contact or a prospective employer, report back, so your initial contact knows you followed through. (Even if the referral didn't lead anywhere, you can say, "Thanks again for introducing me to Leigh Smith. I appreciated being able to contact her.")

And when you do settle into a new job, let all your new and old networking contacts know. Ideally, you'll send one of your new business cards to each person with a note that expresses appreciation for the help provided during your job search.

13. Researching Salaries:
How much can you earn?

Money matters.

When we're in the job market, we want to know how much prospective employers are offering. We want to know what typical raises are. We want to understand bonus criteria, vesting requirements for stock options and benefits plans.

How do you research Seattle-area compensation packages? It's easier to interview well when your initial focus is not money. For that reason, it's important to stay current on compensation trends in your industry and your function, so you'll have a sense of what's reasonable pay. It is also important to recognize that pay here has never been high. Despite low employment and tight regional labor markets in the late 1990s, salaries have remained modest.

According to a late-1997 report by *Marple's Business Newsletter*, "Big pay increases have not materialized except in information systems positions." Quoting Milliman & Robertson, Seattle-based actuaries and consultants, *Marple's* noted, "Companies are under a lot of pressure to contain costs."

Milliman & Robertson also cited the growth in performance-based compensation. Once confined to salespeople or senior executives, bonuses, profit-sharing, stock options and other incentive-pay programs are in many companies now offered to nearly all employees. The incentives may be based on individual or company performance; in some cases, bonuses are paid for individual performance, but only if the company reaches certain profitability levels.

Now, here's some suggestions for researching Puget Sound-area salaries:

SALARY SURVEYS

Milliman & Robertson

1301 Fifth Ave., #3800
Seattle WA 98101
(206) 624-7940

The annual *Northwest Management & Professional Salary Survey* reports base salary and total compensation for more than 150 jobs in Washington and Oregon, including accounting managers, controllers and software programmers. Excludes presidents and CEOs. The employers surveyed are larger firms, both public and private. Cost: $225. More lower-level and technical positions (including webmaster and programmer-analyst) are covered in the *Puget Sound Regional Salary Survey*, which covers jobs in King, Pierce and Snohomish counties. Cost: $225.

Washington Employers
P.O. Box 12068
Seattle WA 98102
(206) 329-1120
Fax: (206) 860-7889
An association that serves small to mid-sized employers (50-200 employees), Washington Employers sells its surveys to nonmembers for $100 per report. Although webmaster is not a job surveyed, the report on office professionals and technical employees includes programmers and systems analysts. Positions such as marketing manager are covered by the *Supervisory and Mid-Management Compensation Survey.*

PROFESSIONAL ASSOCIATIONS

As noted in *Using Professional and Alumni Associations*, some industry groups publish salary information. Often compiled on a national or state basis, much of this information is available only to members; however, certain local associations (for example, the Washington Software & Digital Media Alliance and the Consulting Engineers Council of Washington) do sell copies of their salary surveys to nonmembers. Prices range from $65 to several hundred dollars.

Networking through professional associations and checking their job bank listings is another valuable means of determining salary levels.

EMPLOYMENT AGENCIES AND RECRUITERS

Because they recruit and place employees every day, those agencies that handle temporary, contract and permanent placements often are good sources of information regarding local salary levels. When discussing hourly wages, however, an agency may quote what an employee will be paid (rather than what the client company actually is paying).

Many larger employment agencies have web sites with hourly wages and annual salaries indicated for open positions. For example, when you read *Employment Agencies*, you'll see that salaries for local accounting managers placed by agencies may be about $40,000-$50,000; for controllers, $45,000-$80,000; for legal secretaries, $33,000-$42,000; and for executive secretaries or assistants, $25,000-$50,000. It's important to remember that salaries often depend on the size of a company, whether the work force is unionized and whether the company is publicly held or planning to go public soon.

Some executive search firms provide salary information on their web-site listings of open positions. Among the firms includeed in *Executive Search Firms: Locally Based* that were quoting salaries at press time were Accounting Partners, http://www.apartner.com and Devon James Associates, http://www.devonjames.com.

INVESTOR RELATIONS MATERIAL

Companies that are publicly owned or are offering stock to the public must disclose a limited amount of information about the compensation of the most senior executives. This is helpful if you are seeking a position at that level, either in a particular company or in companies of comparable size in the same business. For a company that has already issued stock, you'll find this information in the annual report and proxy statement. Companies planning to issue stock must publish a prospectus, which will also indicate the compensation of top management. You can obtain such information from a company's investor relations department or on the Securities and Exchange Commission's web site (http://www.sec.gov).

JOB ANNOUNCEMENTS

Reading job postings is an excellent way to conduct your own casual survey of salaries and to compare your credentials with those sought by employers.

Many senior-level positions are advertised in the *Wall Street Journal's* regional edition. Other job postings can be found on employers' and executive search firms' own web sites and in professional association and alumni job-search bulletins. Although many such postings simply indicate "competitive" salary and benefits, government postings almost always include a salary range.

Index

Resume Critique Offer

How good is your resume? What could you do to improve it? If you'd like the opinion of an expert, take advantage of our special resume critique offer for buyers of this book.

Since the publication of the first edition of **How To Find A Good Job In Seattle,** Linda Carlson has spoken to thousands of job-seekers. The most common question: how to write an effective resume. If you have similar concerns, you can now receive a written critique of your resume—for only $15.

To obtain your critique, please send the following:

one neatly typed copy of your resume

the original (no photocopies) of this page

as proof of purchase, your sales receipt for the book. (If your book was purchased by mail and you do not have a receipt, you may substitute a copy of your cancelled check.)

a $15 check made payable in U.S. funds to Barrett Street Productions.

Send all material with a large (No. 10-size or 5 x 7-inch) self-addressed, stamped envelope to:

Resume Critique Offer
Barrett Street Productions
P.O. Box 99642
Seattle WA 98199

You'll receive written comments within six weeks. Caution: marginal notes will be made on the resume you submit. Do not send your only copy. If you'd like critiques of a cover letter, a second version of your resume or a friend's resume, please enclose $15 for each additional item sent at the same time. We're sorry; telephone, fax and e-mail critiques are not available. Resumes submitted without proof of purchase, fee or self-addressed envelope **will not** be critiqued or returned.

Name:_____

Where you purchased your copy of this book (store name and city):

_____

This offer expires Dec. 31, 2000.

How To Save Money On
Your Next Copy Of This Book

To make the next edition of **Executive Search Firms and Employment Agencies in Seattle** even better, we'd appreciate your comments. You need not identify yourself, but if you do, we'll send you a discount coupon worth $10 off either your next copy of this book or a copy of **How to Find a Good Job in Seattle**. Your completed survey should be sent to:

Barrett Street Productions
P.O. Box 99642
Seattle WA 98199

Please tell us where you bought your copy of **Executive Search Firms and Employment Agencies in Seattle**:

_____bookstore _____ by direct mail from_____

Other:_____

Your home ZIP code:_____

If you are not a Puget Sound area resident, do you plan to move here?

____ yes

____ no

Please describe yourself:
_____ seeking professional/technical position
_____ seeking middle management position
_____ seeking senior management or executive position
_____ seeking contract professional or interim management work
_____ seeking secretarial/clerical/administrative position
_____ seeking part-time, temporary or seasonal work
_____ employed, seeking sales leads
_____ job-search counselor
Other:_____

Your age:
____ younger than 25
____ 25-34
____ 34-45
____ 46-55
____ older than 55

Your education level:
____ high school graduate
____ vocational/technical training
____ some college
____ college graduate
____ some postgraduate education
____ postgraduate degree (J.D., M.D., M.S., M.A., M.B.A., etc.)

Your annual household income:
____ less than $25,000
____ $25,000-$40,000
____ $40,000-$55,000
____ $55,000-$100,000
____ more than $100,000

What did you find most valuable about **Executive Search Firms and Employment Agencies in Seattle** ?

Would you recommend it to others?

How would you suggest we improve this book?

To obtain your discount coupon, please enclose:

　　　your sales receipt or other proof of purchase and

　　　a stamped, self-addressed envelope.

Name_____

Address_____

Discount coupons are sent upon receipt of completed surveys only. Please submit the original of this page; no photocopies can be accepted. **Requests cannot be processed without proof of purchase.** One coupon per household. Publisher reserves the right to limit recipients of coupons. Coupons are valid only on books ordered directly from publisher; discounts may not be combined. This offer expires Dec. 31, 2000.